SIC SEMPER TYRANNIS

Why John Wilkes Booth
Shot Abraham Lincoln

William L. Richter

iUniverse, Inc.
New York   Bloomington

Sic Semper Tyrannis
Why John Wilkes Booth Shot Abraham Lincoln

iUniverse books may be ordered through booksellers or by contacting:

iUniverse
1663 Liberty Drive
Bloomington, IN 47403
www.iuniverse.com
1-800-Authors (1-800-288-4677)

ISBN: 978-1-4401-7026-3 (pbk)
ISBN: 978-1-4401-7027-0 (ebook)

Printed in the United States of America

iUniverse rev. date: 9/17/09

Contents

ACKNOWLEDGEMENTS

Thanks to Laurie Verge and Susan Perrotta and the members of the Surratt Society for their invitation to read the first two chapters at their annual meetings in 2005 and 2006. Special thanks to Joseph E. "Rick" Smith III for reading and editing parts of the text and suggesting the cover.

PREFACE

On December 20, 1860, with the secession of South Carolina from the Union, the Unites States died. At least, the American Republic, represented by the Founding Fathers, the Declaration of Independence of 1776, the Articles of Confederation of 1781, and the Constitution of 1787, perished.

But that is not the story modern Americans know. Instead, we are taught that the fraud of secession and the sham of the Confederacy were defeated by the noble President Abraham Lincoln, and the Union was saved through a New Birth of Freedom. Then, at the hour of his triumph, Lincoln's personal victory was spoiled by a mentally unbalanced actor and Southern sympathizer, John Wilkes Booth.

But what if the "accepted" story is wrong? What if President Lincoln's modern reputation is a Yankee fabrication to justify an unjust war? What if John Wilkes Booth were not merely a misguided racist? What if he were not the craziest of what historian and family biographer Stanley Kimmel once called the "Mad Booths of Maryland." What if John Wilkes Booth were a rational man?

The three essays that embraced within this book invite you, the reader, to suspend your belief, if only for a few moments, in the "traditional view" of American history and to look at Abraham Lincoln and John Wilkes Booth from a new and different perspective. The notion that Booth might have had legitimate reasons for hating Lincoln is not new. But the tying of this hatred to commonly held Southern theories about American government and the Constitution of the time are unique.

The first essay presents a President Lincoln that was familiar to Americans before Republican propaganda made him into a demigod. The second shows John Wilkes Booth as an ordinary Southerner, very much a man of his time, holding to a cooperationist political philosophy, which was very common in the South before the Civil War. The final essay presents Booth's transformation into a secessionist and then a tyrannicide.

Booth and the South fell into a unique gap in American history. In reality, there are two Americas;

there is the United States before Lincoln (typified by the phrase "the United States *are*"), a federal republic guaranteed by the written Constitution, and the United States after Lincoln (typified by the phrase "the United States *is*"), an empire under a "living" Constitution, that means nothing more than the current generation of the ruling class says it does.

Under the empire that Lincoln and the Republican party created with their victory at Appomattox by defeating the American South, the new United States went forth to conquer the American West, "civilize" Asia and the Caribbean, and subdue the world with our industrial production enhanced by American victories in two World Wars and numerous police actions that destroyed our enemies and allies alike. Not until the tragedies of Viet Nam and the assassination of President John F. Kennedy did Abraham Lincoln's American empire know defeat.[1]

There were setbacks here and there.[2] They were especially notable every twenty years, like clockwork

---

1   The concept of the American growth to world power is a theme from Victor Davis Hanson, "Presidents Aren't What They Used to Be," July 16, 2009, Jewish World Review,com/0709/hanson071609.php3. For the South as an exception to the rule of progress, see C. Vann Woodward, "The Irony of Southern History," *Journal of Southern History*, 19 (1953), 3-19.

2   Some of these problems are discussed in C. Vann Woodward, "A Second Look at the Theme of Irony," in

starting in 1840, marring the seemingly inevitable American march of progress. These were the sudden deaths of seven presidents, three from natural causes, and four more, beginning with Lincoln, from violence.

Come with us then back to those halcyon days of yesteryear, when the United States was still a republic; to a time before it became an empire. Let's look into the mind of the man who became a scapegoat at the altar of Abraham Lincoln, the president whom modern historians regularly praise as the greatest American who ever lived. Let's take a fresh look at President Lincoln's assassin; that man condemned as the most demented of the Mad Booths of Maryland. What on earth could have motivated John Wilkes Booth to shoot Abraham Lincoln, the alleged architect of all that made America great?

Woodward (ed.), *The Burden of Southern History* (New York: Mentor, 1969, rev. ed.), 150-62.

I.

How Did Anakin Skywalker Become Darth Vader? The Abraham Lincoln John Wilkes Booth Knew[1]

In an interview with *Time* Magazine, noted film producer and director George Lucas of *Star Wars* fame explored how he envisioned an electoral republic becoming a dictatorial empire. Expanding on a theme first coined by Benjamin Franklin ("Those who would give up essential liberty to obtain a little temporary safety deserve neither liberty nor safety"),[2] Lucas' contention was that the people voluntarily grant a leader, the man on a white horse, if you will, despotic powers, selling off their liberties for security. "It isn't that the Empire conquers the Republic,

---

1 This question was asked in a more general form leaving out the reference to Abraham Lincoln by George Lukas in an interview with *Time*, 159 (No. 17, April 29, 2002), 56-66, especially 65, quoted in David Dieteman, "Episode II: Art Imitates Life," at http://www.lewrockwell.com/kinglincolnarchive.

2 Jay Winik, "Security Comes Before Liberty," *Wall Street Journal* (October 23, 2001), disagrees with Franklin and is taken to task for it in Jeff Dantré, "A Sad and Shocking Commentary," at www.lewrockwell.com/orig2/dantre1.html.

it's that the Empire *is* the Republic," Lucas said. More important, as a part of his celluloid study, Lucas took a look at how an individual goes bad and sells his soul to the new order--the tale of how the noble Jedi knight of the Republic, Anakin Skywalker, morphed into the evil lord of the Empire, Darth Vader.

Lucas was not engaging in an idle exercise in semantics or fiction with his on-screen speculations. In the past decades, American historians and journalists have been doing exactly same thing in print with none other than Abraham Lincoln. In the process of exploring Lincoln and his goals and objectives and intended or unintended results in fighting the American Civil War, the allegedly humble, small-time railroad lawyer, who became America's first Republican president, has historiographically gone from hero to villain. In Lucas' terms, Lincoln has been transformed from Anakin Skywalker—the Lincoln we know-- into Darth Vader—the Lincoln John Wilkes Booth knew.

It has not been an easy metamorphosis. In the words of one commentator, "For whatever reason, it strikes a nerve when esteemed politicians like Abe Lincoln . . . are criticized. . . . People do not like to see their heroes tarnished." Indeed, the Lincolnites, defined by one disgruntled critic as "those empowered to tell the rest of us rubes what everything really means,"[3] would maintain that the transformation has not taken place. They have a point. Americans traditionally have been and are infected with something best called "acute Lincolnitis."[4] As one writer described it, "After the fall of the Roman Republic, the citizens of Rome were encouraged to worship their caesars as gods. The United States is little different. Rather than Caesar Augustus or Gaius Caligula, Americans (particularly up North) are raised in the Cult of Saint Lincoln."[5] In the more measured opinion of his epic biographer, fellow Illinoisan Carl Sandburg, of all the participants in the Civil War era, "[n]one threw a longer shadow than [Abraham Lincoln]."[6]

But Sandburg was being modest in his claim. More often, Lincoln, whom James Russell Lowell characterized as the first real American (born in Kentucky, raised in Indiana, matured in Illinois, and possessing the soul and truth of a Massachusetts man, as another writer clarified

---

3   David Dieteman, "Unpleasant Truths," and Clyde Wilson, "DiLorenzo and His Critics," *ibid.*
4   Myles Cantor, "Charles Kesler's Lincolnitis," *ibid.*
5   David Dieteman, "LBJ, FDR, and Lincoln: Peas in a Pod," *ibid.*
6   Carl Sandburg, *Abraham Lincoln: The Prairie Years and the War Years* (3 vols., abridged, New York: Dell, 1959), III, 885.

it), [7] is commonly seen as so crucial to America's past, present, and future that historian David H. Donald, thirty years before he penned what is arguably the best one-volume history of the Northern Civil War leader,[8] wrote a pivotal essay, "Getting Right with Lincoln."[9]

By his title, Donald meant that Americans of all political persuasions (even the U.S. Communist Party)

---

7   James Russell Lowell, "Ode Recited at the Harvard Commemoration [July 21, 1865]," *Atlantic Monthly*, 16 (September 1865), 364-71, Canto VI, line 208, as characterized in Edgar Lee Masters, *Lincoln, the Man* (New York: Dodd, Mead & Company, 1931), 455.

8   David H. Donald, *Lincoln* (New York: Simon & Schuster, 1995). The other contenders for best one volume biography are Benjamin P. Thomas, *Abraham Lincoln* (New York: Knopf, 1952); and Stephen B. Oates, *With Malice Toward None: The Life of Abraham Lincoln* (New York: Harper & Row, 1977). The current definitive Lincoln biography is Michael Burlingame's massive two volume effort, *Abraham Lincoln: A Life* (Baltimore: The Johns Hopkins University Press, 2008).

9   David H. Donald, "Getting Right with Lincoln, in Donald (ed.), *Lincoln Reconsidered: Essays on the Civil War Period* (New York: Vintage, 1956), 3-18, which is complemented by T. Harry Williams, "Abraham Lincoln: Principle and Pragmatism in Politics," *Mississippi Valley Historical Review*, 40 (June 1953), 89-108. For a recent statement of getting right with Lincoln, see Mario Coumo, *Why Lincoln Matters Today More than Ever* (New York: Harcourt, 2004), with commentary by Chuck Colson, "Why Lincoln Matters," September 3, 2004, www.townhall.com.

like to see their positions on any and every issue as the one that Abraham Lincoln, America's best-loved, highest-rated President, would have held were he alive today. In his essay, Donald posited that the reason for this "getting right with Lincoln" was that Lincoln was not only a very capable chief executive, but a very practical president, qualities that have marked all great American heads of state from George Washington to the present.

Lincoln put it more bluntly, "[m]y policy is to have no policy." Rather, he constantly sought to "rise above principle and embrace practicality," to borrow a phrase that another admiring Lincoln scholar, the late T. Harry Williams, liked to tweak his Louisiana State University graduate students with in years past. Williams' and Donald's point was that Lincoln was very non-ideological. He followed Thomas Jefferson's time-honored dictum that "politics is the art of the possible." It is a very American approach to problem-solving at all levels. Even today, being in league with Lincoln is a great vote-getter.

This characterization of Lincoln as the great practical man, whom all Americans (regardless of political antecedents, Union or Confederate, Republican or Democrat, Independent or Communist), wish and need to be in step with, immediately put those who questioned or opposed him be they John Wilkes Booth, Northern and Southern Democrats, the advocates of the

Constitution as it was before Lincoln's accession to power (all of which can be summed up in the hackneyed phrase Rum, Romanism, and Rebellion) at a real disadvantage. It has not done much for historians who challenge Lincoln's role in American History, either, as Montgomery S. Lewis' bluntly titled volume, *Legends that Libel Lincoln* (1946) aptly demonstrated.[10] Critics take on the massive Lincoln historical machine, "a formidable and intimidating task," opined historian Robert W. Johannsen,[11] at great risk to their own reputations.

Nonetheless, the attack on Lincoln's historical celebrity has taken place on several fronts: one led by white historians like Edgar Lee Masters and Melvin Eustace Bradford; another by African American magazine editor and historian Lerone Bennett, Jr.; and the most recent by white economist and historian Thomas J. DiLorenzo.[12] Actually, there are close to seventy articles

---

10   Montgomery S. Lewis, *Legends that Libel Lincoln* (New York: Rinehart & Co., 1946).

11   Robert W. Johanssen, *Lincoln, the South, and Slavery* (Baton Rouge: Louisiana State University Press, 1990), as quoted in Thomas J. DiLorenzo, *The Real Lincoln: A New Look at Abraham Lincoln, His Agenda, and an Unnecessary War* (Roseville, CA.: Forum, 2002), 1.

12   Each of these men writes from a slightly different perspective. Masters represents a Populist-Progressive viewpoint. Bradford is within the Southern Conservative tradition. Bennett is modern left wing Civil Rights advocate. DiLorenzo tends toward modern libertarianism.

and several books that challenge Lincoln's historical reputation, which has become an industry in itself. But these four present the root arguments that others have built upon.[13]

Although there were hints that the Lincoln story was not all the public might think in early works by William H. Herndon[14] and Albert J. Beveridge[15], the first prominent writer to challenge the Lincoln Myth openly was Edgar Lee Masters. Born in Kansas, Masters read law at his father's Chicago law office, and lived in

---

For a discussion of Bradford and Bennett see, Dinesh D'Souza, "Lincoln: Tyrant, Hypocrite, or Consummate Statesman?" *American History Magazine*, at historynet. com/ah/bllincolnstatesman/index.html.

13 Most of these articles can be found at http://www. lewrockwell.com/kinglincolnarchive. A good but dated essay on the "Anti-Lincoln Tradition," is in Don E. Fehrrenbacher, *Lincoln in Text and Context: Collected Essays* (Palo Alto: Stanford University Press, 1987), 197-213.

14 William H. Herndon and Jesse W. Weik, *Life of Lincoln* (Edited by Paul W. Angle, Cleveland: World Publishing Company, 1942, orig. 1888). A listing of favorable Lincoln biographies, what some might call the "Lincoln Juggernaut," can be found in Fehrenbacher, "The Changing Image of Lincoln in American Historiography," *Lincoln in Text and Context*, 181-96. For a more complete listing of works on Lincoln, consult Michael Burkhimer, *100 Essential Lincoln Books* (Nashville: Cumberland House Publishing, 2003).

15 Albert J. Beveridge, *Abraham Lincoln, 1809-1858* (2 vols., Boston: Houghton Mifflin Company 1928).

Illinois. A life-long Democrat, raised in the Progressive tradition that epitomized the eras of Theodore Roosevelt and Woodrow Wilson, Masters was a sometime lawyer (a partner of Clarence Darrow in the first decade of the twentieth century before the Scopes "Monkey" Trial), novelist, playwright, and poet (renowned for his *Spoon River Anthology*), who wrote several biographies, one of which was an in-depth study of Abraham Lincoln published in 1931.[16]

Masters began his study by praising Herndon, for having the courage to criticize his old law partner, Lincoln, in 1889,[17] "when partisanship and myth making were at floodtide, repelling all reports that dimmed Lincoln's deification"; and Beveridge (a former U.S. senator from Indiana, Bull Moose Republican, and author of a four volume biography of Chief Justice John Marshall), for confirming Herndon's criticisms of the sixteenth president and "[n]either trying to idealize Lincoln, nor to depreciate him." Since these "authentic" biographers had pretty much exhausted the need to find out more facts about Lincoln, Masters hoped but to "touch" him "with the hand of rational analysis" as to his "mind and character," fully realizing that "numberless writers were

---

16 Edgar Lee Masters, *Lincoln, the Man.*
17 Herndon waited until Mary Lincoln had died in 1882, before putting his research before the public in print.

bent upon giving Lincoln apotheosis, and none that was heeded said anything of influence against him." [18]

Masters' backhanded slap at those who would deify Lincoln was an indirect criticism of his one-time good friend and fellow Chicago writer, Carl Sandburg. Masters believed that his revealing to Sandburg his own plan to write a Lincoln biography had led Sandburg to beat him into print with the first two of his lengthy six volume study of Lincoln, which many believed was truly an attempt to bestow upon Lincoln sainthood through a masterful combination of truth and fiction passing for fact. That Masters did not deign to mention Jesse W. Weik's 1922 volume, probably indicated he saw in it nothing new from Weik's earlier collaborations with Herndon. [19]

Masters revealed his bias when he dedicated his book to Thomas Jefferson, "whose universal genius through a long life was devoted to the peace, enlightenment, and liberty of the Union created by the Constitution of 1787." Admitting that "there was much in [Lincoln] that appealed to the hearts of those who most stoutly

18 *Ibid.,* [iii].
19 Herbert K. Russell, *Edgar Lee Masters: A Biography* (Urbana: University of Illinois Press, 2001), 271-74. See also, Jesse W. Weik, *The Real Lincoln: A Portrait* (Boston: Houghton Mifflin, 1922). Weik had collaborated in three earlier edition's of Herndon's work (1889, 1892 and 1921).

resented his politics," Masters went on to manifest what he called an "emancipated and realistic attitude towards records once touched so gingerly and with such regard to Lincoln as the colossal and sacred figure of a just war waged for liberty!"[20] Masters then challenged Lincoln's historical apotheosis by assailing his personal character, his record on emancipation, his economic policy, his Unconstitutional and illegal centralization of political power in the Federal government, and his insertion of religion and morality into his policy stands.

According to Masters, "Honest Abe" was a political dissembler and equivocator of the highest order. "It may be a vain task to follow the inconstant mind of Lincoln, but at least its vacillations can be recorded," Masters said.[21] Lincoln spoke out against slavery in principle but did nothing against it before the war and little during the conflict. He created a mythical War of Rebellion, when in fact the war was as much for Southern independence as the Revolutionary War had been for division from Great Britain. He concealed his true objective to start a war by insisting that secession in 1860 (in which a state that was free and independent with no U.S. laws operating within its jurisdiction, requiring invasion and attack to subdue it) was the same as nullification in 1832 (where a

---

20 Masters, *Lincoln, the Man*, 1-3.
21 *Ibid.*, 249-50.

state was still within the Union and merely resisting the enforcement of a U.S. law within its boundaries, requiring a *posse commitatus* under U.S. marshals to counter it). Lincoln, who dismissed such technicalities as "pernicious abstraction[s],"[22] intentionally did not appoint new Federal officials to collect U.S. tariffs in Charleston harbor after South Carolina's secession, Masters asserted, but invaded with a Federal naval expedition, starting a war in violation of his pledge in his First Inaugural Speech, which he then artfully blamed on the South.[23]

But there was more, Masters said. At Gettysburg Lincoln erroneously spoke of the Founding Fathers creating a new nation in 1776, when in fact thirteen nations had been created under a formal alliance, a fact recognized by King George III in the Treaty of Paris in 1783. He spoke of a government "of the people, by the people, and for the people," but denied self-determination to the Southern [white] people. "But," as the famous Baltimore cynic and critic of most all other things Southern, H. L. Mencken, warned of the Gettysburg Address in another forum, "let us not forget that it is poetry, not logic; beauty, not sense." Lincoln sanctimoniously called for "malice toward

---

22 Roy P. Basler (ed.), *The Collected Works of Abraham Lincoln* (8 vols. and index, New Brunswick: Rutgers University Press, 1953), VIII, 403.

23 *Ibid.*, 29-30, 41-42, 379-85, 402. The First Inaugural Speech is in Basler (ed.), *Collected Works*, IV, 262-71.

none and charity for all" in his Second Inaugural Speech, Masters went on, as his armies tore a path of pillage and rapine sixty miles wide through Georgia and South Carolina, burning Atlanta and Columbia, and despoiled the Shenandoah Valley of Virginia, without significant opposition.[24] Lincoln rationalized it all by enunciating the "Hebraic-Puritan principle of assuming to act as one's brother's keeper, when the real motive was to become one's brother's jailer," Masters contended.[25]

Echoing Herndon and Beveridge, Masters found Lincoln's dishonesty extended to other realms, such as his relations with women. Herndon believed Lincoln's lifetime melancholy was brought on by his marriage to Mary Todd, whom he characterized as the "female wild cat of the age." To explain this ill-begotten union, Herndon latched on to the Ann Rutledge story, which became sheer poetry in the hands of a master story-teller like Carl Sandburg.[26] But Masters found that Lincoln

---

24 Masters, *Lincoln, the Man*, 397, 456-62, 471, 487-79. For the Mencken comments, see *Smart Set*, (May 1920), 141. The Gettysburg speech is in Basler (ed.), *Collected Works*, VII, 23; and the Second Inaugural speech in *ibid.*, VIII, 332-33.

25 Masters, *Lincoln, the Man*, 479.

26 Donald, "Herndon and Mrs. Lincoln," *Lincoln Reconsidered*, 37-56, especially 44; Herndon and Jesse W. Weik, *Life of Lincoln* , 110-15; and Sandburg, *Abraham Lincoln*, I, 75-77, 85-90.

never had much of a relationship with Ann at all. Indeed she was betrothed to another and not impressed with the Railsplitter one iota. Lincoln's attempt to hook up with another local belle, Mary Owens, brought about a flat "no." As she later explained, "I thought Mr. Lincoln was deficient in those little links which make up the chain of a woman's happiness--at least it was so in my case." Then Lincoln proved her correct by cruelly making fun of her physical attributes to his friends.[27]

Masters theorized that after that rejection, Lincoln espoused Mary Todd for her money and because it was the thing to do--to have a wife at his age.[28] But he hemmed and hawed his way into matrimony, tended to stay away from home unduly, and never wrote her a warm letter or acted as if he cared that much. This has led moderns to assert that Lincoln evidenced too many homosexual traits, and a suspicious, close relationship with roommate Joshua Speed, and later with an avowedly homosexual army captain during the war, to be anything but bisexual.[29] Actually, to a large degree, this accusation

27 Thomas Fleming, "Lincoln's Tragic Heroism," *National Review*, 31 (December 8, 1989), 39-40.

28 Masters, *Lincoln, the Man* , 45-57-8, 60-76.

29 W. Scott Thompson, "Was Lincoln Gay?" at http://hnn. us/articles/96.html. The homosexual traits Thompson lists are bonded relationships with other men, absence of attraction to women, a bad marriage revolving around the absence of sex, effeminate characteristics (Lincoln liked to

pardon people), and rumors (where there is smoke there is fire). Thompson believes that three of five is prima facie case for homosexuality. See also, letters between Philip Nobile and Gabor S. Boritt and Peter Ginna at http://hnn.us/articles/96.html. Boritt dismisses the stories of Lincoln's homosexuality in his *The Lincoln Enigma* (New York: Oxford University Press, 2001), xiv-xvi. See also Jonah Goldberg, "The Goldberg File: Abe's Been Outed," at www.nationalreview.com/goldberg/goldbergo50499.html, whose basic argument on Lincoln's sexual preferences is, "so what?" For more, see also, "Was Abe Lincoln Gay? The Blockbuster Book That Will Change America's History," by Doug Ireland, *LA Weekly Press*, Oct 29-Nov 4 2004, reviewed forthcoming volume by C.A. Tripp, *The Intimate World of Abraham Lincoln* (New York: Free Press 2005). In passing, Ireland mentioned allegedly previously invisible homosexual companions and love objects of America's sixteenth president. Among them were Henry C. Whitney; the young Billy Greene, a Salem contemporary of Lincoln's and another bedmate (who supposedly admired Lincoln's thighs); Nat Grigsby; and A.Y. Ellis. Two early mentions of Lincoln's bisexuality are Lieutenant Colonel Thomas Chamberlin, *History of the One hundred and Fiftieth Regiment, Pennsylvania Volunteers. Second Regiment, Bucktail Brigade*. (Philadelphia, J. B. Lippincott company, 1895). Chamberlin spoke of Lincoln's alleged well-known tryst in the White House in 1863 with Captain David Derickson, one of Chamberlin's subordinates. Arguably Lincoln's most famous biographer, Carl Sandburg, *The Prairie Years* (2 vols., 1926), I, 264, 266 , refers to Lincoln's four-year relationship with Joshua Speed as being characterized by "a streak of lavender and spots soft as May violets." Jim Kepner, editor of *ONE*, an early gay magazine, the historian of gay America Jonathan Ned Katz *Love Stories: Sex between Men before*

against Lincoln was answered decades before it became trendy in William Herndon's *Life of Lincoln* (Lincoln courted three women and married another) and William E. Barton's volume, *The Women Who Loved Lincoln*.[30] But "[h]is attitude toward women to the last day of his

Homosexuality. (Chicago: University of Chicago Press, 2001), and University of Massachusetts professor Charley Shively, "Big Buck & Big Lick: Abe Lincoln & Walt Whitman", in Winston Leyland, *Gay Roots : Twenty Years of Gay Sunshine :An Anthology of Gay History, Sex, Politics, and Culture* (San Francisco : Gay Sunshine Press, 1991), 125-37, all refer to these and other so-called incidents. The most complete discussion of Lincoln's bi-sexual preferences is in C. A. Tripp, *The Intimate World of Abraham Lincoln* (New York: Free Press 2004). Finally, Gore Vidal has said in interviews that, in researching his historical novel on Lincoln, he began to suspect that Lincoln was a same-sexer.

30 Herndon as paraphrased in Richard N. Current, *The Lincoln Nobody Knows* (New York: Hill & Wang, 1963), 37. But of 11 informants Herndon used to write his Life of Lincoln, only one, Judge David B. Davis, thought of Lincoln as a skirt chaser, saying only Lincoln's self-control saved many a woman from conquest. Douglas O. Wilson and Rodney O. Davis (eds.), *Herndon's Informants: Letters, Interviews, and Statements about Abraham Lincoln* (Urbana: University of Illinois Press, 1998), 91-92, 105, 108, 131, 170-71, 350, 373-74, 443, 455, 518, 541. See also, William E. Barton, *The Women Who Loved Lincoln* (Indianapolis: Bobbs-Merrill Company, 1927). As an aside, anyone who has not seen the beautiful picture of Mary Todd at age twenty that is the frontispiece of Barton's work, needs to. One glance explains why every man in Springfield chased her.

life was but a continuation of his boyhood diffidence," Masters concluded, describing Lincoln's relations with women, in a word, as "undersexed."[31]

Indeed, Masters found Lincoln to be a "cold man" in general, referring to acquaintances (except for Herndon, whom he called "Billy") solely by their family names. Masters compared him to the icy French revolutionary leader Maximilien Robespierre, but possessing a marvelous sense of humor. This, combined with "his intellectual and critical faculties, coupled . . . with a sort of sluggishness and indifference," which Masters blamed on a slow liver, intestinal toxaemia, and sedentary habits, created a man ordinarily full of "black despondency," who gloried in cruel, insensible tales of the destruction of the South, dismissing the hundred of thousands of casualties as God's will, "though the whole land be made one tomb." But Lincoln's psyche was tempered with a strange duality, Masters said. He also had a bright side, as seen in his assertion of "with malice toward none."[32]

Like Lincoln's personal traits, Masters found his record on freeing the slaves to be less than his reputation as the Great Emancipator. Lincoln's public utterances on slavery began with what Masters dismissed as "[t]he pleasant story" that Lincoln allegedly told his cousin

---

31 Masters, *Lincoln, the Man*, 20, 145.
32 *Ibid.*, 139, 140, 142, 143, 145, 244, 427, 429, 431.

Dennis Hanks around the time he took a raft down to New Orleans and saw the institution first-hand. According to Hanks, Lincoln said that if he ever had a chance he would hit slavery hard. With that in mind, he and another Illinois legislator introduced a nice-sounding, do-nothing resolution against slavery in the state legislature in 1837.

But, according to Masters, by 1854, Lincoln had not gone much further. His heart was divided between opposition to slavery and allegiance to the law, and he did not know how to resolve the dilemma. As a congressman, Lincoln voted for the Wilmot Proviso, which called for making all the land obtained from Mexico in the Mexican-American War free territory. But he also voted against limiting slavery or repealing the slave code in the District of Columbia, spoke out on behalf of enforcing the Fugitive Slave Acts, and publicly denied that he was for giving black men the vote, the right to hold public office or sit on juries, the right to intermarry with whites, the right to use public accommodations.[33]

At least that is what he said in southern Illinois, the fabled "Little Egypt." But in Yankee-dominated northern Illinois, Lincoln talked differently, a fact pointed out with glee in debate by his opponent for the United States senate seat in 1858, Stephen A. Douglas. Basically

---

33 *Ibid.*, 24, 96, 100, 235.

Lincoln wanted to free the slaves and allow them to enter the labor force to earn a living, but they were to be kept subordinate to the white race in all matters in perpetuity, because of perceived physical differences. Lincoln wanted the African American to enjoy life, liberty, and the pursuit of happiness, in his or her place, but not in the Great West, competing side by side with white labor. As Masters said, "in the roar of the incoming tide of destiny the absurdities of Lincoln's philosophizations have been drowned; but for a study of Lincoln's mind nothing better shows its incoherence" than his stand on slavery.[34]

When Lincoln announced the preliminary Emancipation Proclamation in late 1862, Masters said, he was hoping to hold the Republican majority in Congress. His implementation of the Proclamation in January 1863 was not a seizure of property, but the urging of domestic slave rebellion. As president, Masters maintained, Lincoln took no oath to preserve the Union or end slavery. He took an oath to protect the Constitution. "To destroy the Constitution to save the Union was like saving the Union at the expense of any solution on slavery, whether by total, partial, or no emancipation," Masters concluded. In the end, Lincoln showed that he too had some reservations about declaring emancipation as part of a military policy through an executive proclamation.

---

34 *Ibid.*, 148, 303-11.

His hope was that Congress would enact compensated emancipation instead.[35]

As with emancipation, Masters saw Lincoln's economic policy full of contradictions. Far from being the little man's president as reputed, Lincoln supported and was "supported by great wealth." From his first days in 1832 at New Salem, Illinois, to the end of his life, Lincoln supported the party of privilege and monopoly in the Antebellum Era, the Whigs. "It is something requiring explanation," Masters contended, "that Lincoln, who is held up as an apostle of liberty, who himself along the way said so much of the Declaration of Independence and Jefferson, turned in his youth to the rhetorician [and Whig Party leader] Henry Clay and clung to him into maturity, and followed his lead essentially to the end." [36]

"Clay was the champion of that political system which doles out favors to the strong in order to keep their adherence to the government," Masters said. He explained this by the fact that Lincoln was ashamed of the poverty of his youth and moved as an adult to be one of, and associate with, the rich. While there are many tales of Lincoln defending the poor in court, his real income came from being a corporate lawyer, the representative of the Illinois Central Railroad which drove squatters and

35 *Ibid.,* 317, 435, 437, 439, 453-54.
36 *Ibid.,* 3, 4, 26.

settlers, like the Lincoln family of his youth, from their desired rights of way.

Masters saw Lincoln as essentially a lazy attorney who relied on his partner, Billy Herndon, to do all the leg work on a case. Then Lincoln, who always had the ability to move an audience, would sway the jury. Masters accused Lincoln of being essentially indolent, lying on the couch, regaling loafers with witty stories, dabbling in local politics, "indisposed to undertake anything that savored of exertion." Masters notes that the Lincoln estate in 1865 was worth $100,000, but he implied it should have been more, since only Herndon did the work, an impression that has since been refuted by the publication of Lincoln's Legal Papers, which show that he averaged over 200 cases a years for twenty-five years.[37]

Lincoln's laziness made him not an original thinker, Masters claimed. For this he relied economically on Henry Clay's American System. This was a program, originally developed by economist Matthew Carey (Clay was an indolent thinker, too), that promoted a national banking system, internal improvements, and the

---

37 *Ibid.*, 11, 13, 84, 116, 118, 122, 141. See also, Martha L Benner and Cullom Davis (eds.), *The Law Practice of Abraham Lincoln: Complete Documentary Edition* (3 DVDs, Champaign: University of Illinois Press, 2000). See also, Gerald J. Prokopowicz, "'A Superior Opportunity of Being a Good Man," at http://www.papersofabrahamlincoln. org/DEReview.htm.

liberation of American slaves and their return to Africa. Clay originally hoped to finance this with a high tariff designed to exclude foreign imports and the sale of land in the western territories at $1.25 an acre. But by the 1850s, the notion of land sales had evaporated in favor of homesteading the land for free, causing the rest of the program to rely on the tariff alone for its financing--a tariff paid predominantly by the South, which imported European goods in exchange for its cotton.[38]

It was for this reason that Lincoln refused to join the initially antislavery Republican Party, Masters contended. Until it adopted the American System, which had been continually rejected by the American voter from Thomas Jefferson to James Buchanan, the Republicans had little to offer Whigs like Lincoln. But once this was achieved by 1856, Masters explained, Lincoln and the Republican Party were "chiefly concerned with letting in a new set of thieves to the public treasury . . . , but they came in [through the election of 1860] under the guise of piety and humanitarianism." The Republicans then proceeded to loot the nation during the hostilities and the Reconstruction that followed under the cover of a war to liberate the slaves and preserve the Union.

---

38 Masters, *Lincoln, the Man*, 122, 297. For the American System, see Glyndon G. Van Deusen, *The Jacksonian Era, 1828-1848* (New York: Harper & Row, Publishers, 1959), 51.

Although Lincoln himself seemed personally honest, much like U. S. Grant who followed him, he turned a blind eye to what was happening. But he did see to it Congress enacted the American System, the basis of the corruption, which he signed. And he kept the war going, refusing all attempts at compromise. "The reason [was] that [Lincoln and] the master minds of the Republican Party, the offshoots of [Henry Clay], had for further purposes, seeing the capitalistic advantages that now revealed themselves," Masters said. "They cared nothing for the Union compared to what they cared for money and power."[39]

Money and power. That brought Masters to what he called Lincoln's unconstitutional and illegal centralization of political authority in the Federal government, which Masters embodied in one word--despotism. From the time of Jefferson, Masters wrote, for over fifty years, republican principles of state sovereignty and government of the people had held sway over the American government. "But all the while," Masters asserted conspiratorially, "a patient, secret, self-conscious influence was gathering power"--he called its believers "mongrel breeds"--"appropriating it from the people and the states and storing it in a central government for the

---

39 Masters, *Lincoln, the Man*, 214-32, 444-45, 446, 483, 487.

purposes of business and money, and under the guise of law and order, of religion, and even of liberty." From the very first Lincoln "was a centralist, a privilegist, an adherent of the non-principled Whig Party, which had laid the foundation of the Republican Party," Masters said.[40]

Lincoln's Illinois opponent for the U.S. senate seat in 1858, Stephen A. Douglas, tried to warn the voters what Lincoln was about during the Lincoln-Douglas debate at Chicago. He believed that the American system would have to impose a uniformity upon the states from Washington, D.C. to function. Deep in its haughty plans, Douglas said, was a hidden agenda to abolish the state legislatures, blot out state sovereignty, merge the rights and sovereignty of the (then) thirty-two states into one consolidated empire, and vest the Federal government with state police power and the right to make all domestic law.

This was in violation of the cardinal instruction of American government, Masters stated, where the state legislatures are constituent assemblies that can pass any law not expressly prohibited by state and Federal Constitutions, while Congress is not a constituent assembly and can pass only those laws warranted by an actual grant of power from the states in the Federal

---

40 *Ibid*, 497.

Constitution (there were no implied powers in Master's eyes). There would be a uniformity of despotism throughout the land, Masters claimed, "exactly what the plutocratic interests of the time wished, and they were deploying the abolitionists, who knew nothing about the nature of the Union and cared less, to bring this consideration about."[41]

The result, according to Masters, was a bevy of unconstitutional Lincolnian acts in response to the secession of the South that "are glossed over with the remark that what he did before Congress met on July 4, 1861, was validated by that Congress and made lawful for his great purpose of saving the Union." But Lincoln acted during that time and others intentionally when Congress was out of session as "an emperor with full despotic power and his rightful masters had had no word to say about it." He ruled exactly as did the British King Charles I or Oliver Cromwell--without Parliament. [42]

Lincoln increased the size of the regular army, Masters said, circumvented Congress by calling up the militia and volunteers with the connivance of Republican state governors, spent funds appropriated for one governmental agency in another, suspended the writ of habeas corpus, replaced civil courts with military

---

41 *Ibid.,* 302, 345.
42 *Ibid.,* 113, 373, 399-400.

commissions, imposed an illegal blockade against the South, declared privateers with letters of marque to be pirates (the Declaration of Paris in 1865 had outlawed privateers, but the U.S. had failed to sign on), arrested suspect members of the Maryland state legislature to guarantee a Union majority, ignored a decision of the Chief Justice of the United States Supreme court while riding circuit, created a national police force to enforce loyalty, and invaded a foreign land. "It was a *coup d'etat* in every essential feature," Masters complained, "a government made a nation from a confederacy of states by the glorious acts of an army headed by Lincoln." In Masters' most consummate statement, "the Constitution . . . was shot to death at Gettysburg."[43]

Why do we hear so little of this travesty? one might ask. The history of the United States is written by those who do not understand the constitutional relationships of a confederated republic, Masters would answer. These "twistifications" (Masters used Jefferson's word to describe the centralizing tendencies of those like Alexander Hamilton, John Marshall, Henry Clay, and Abraham Lincoln), allowed Republicans to apply "a higher law than the Constitution," in the phrase of Lincoln's Secretary of State, William H. Seward.[44]

---

43 *Ibid.*, 4, 398-414, 422.
44 *Ibid.*, 81, 197.

Lincoln's willingness to be associated with "higher law" doctrine allowed him to ally his trampling of the Constitution and law with the purpose of God, Masters grumped.[45] It is not that Lincoln was particularly religious in his own life. Stepmother Sarah Bush Johnston said that Lincoln had no religion as a boy, never talked about religion, and as far as she could observe did not even think about religion. In his new Salem days Lincoln wrote an essay against the Bible and challenged its being God's revelations to man. He also strove to prove that Jesus was not the son of God. Lincoln was so open on this as to be charged with being an atheist by political opponents and friends alike.

But Masters found that Lincoln was "immersed in Hebraic-Christianity from his earliest years which is something deeper than belonging to a church or professing a creed. He was a Jehovah [Old Testament] man all his life; and he early realized the advantage of using the Bible for his appeals to the people." Indeed, Masters claimed that "Lincoln was the first president to invest the government with Christianity and to put its poisonous inoculation deep down in the flesh of the Republic."

Masters went on to assert that "in Lincoln's case the subjugation of the South had to be smeared over with

---

45 *Ibid.*, 81-82.

religion, . . . with the whole rank and file of Calvinism, with the nauseating piety and sadistic righteousness of America as a Christian nation. . . . The War Between the States was for God," Masters said, "and Lincoln made it so. But there was nothing in Lincoln's philosophy which forbade riches and privileges; rather the contrary. Hence he laid the foundation for . . . missions of irreverence and plunder." Masters adjudged that Lincoln was truly America's patron saint of despotism, big business, and hypocrisy. "[I]t is not for lack of facts that the myths have grown up about Lincoln," Masters concluded. "The facts have been disregarded in order that the portrait of him might be drawn that American wanted."[46]

Needless to say, the public went berserk upon the book's publication in 1931. Masters, in effect, told them that a valued part of their past was a sham. *Time* magazine coined a new word to describe Masters, "Lincolnoclast." The *New York Times Book Review* labeled called his book, "A Belittling Life of Lincoln by Edgar Lee Masters." The rival *New York Telegram* wailed in astonishment, "Lincoln Killed Our Freedom, Says Masters." A bill was introduced in Congress to prohibit mailing the book as it was "lewd, obscene, lascivious, filthy, and indecent." The volume was

---

46 *Ibid.*, 21, 34, 124, 149, 150, 151, 154-56, 480, 490, 491, 493-94.

banned in Boston, the height of moral condemnation in the 1930s.

His hometown of Petersburg, Illinois, seriously thought of removing Masters' "Spoon River" epitaph from Ann Rutledge's tombstone, until they found that she probably was not buried there--at least there were no bones, just four worn dress buttons in the grave. Even the Knights of the Ku Klux Klan lambasted him and warned that they had their eyes upon him, although God only knows why. On the other hand, the Sons of Confederate Veterans praised the book highly. In the end, Masters' reputation was damaged beyond salvation, while Carl Sandburg's competing effort became the new Lincoln best-selling standard.[47]

But despite Masters' fate, there were others who would willingly apply for the job of Chief Lincolnoclast. One of these was Melvin Eustace Bradford. Son of a West Texas rancher, Bradford was educated at the University of Oklahoma and Vanderbilt University. At the latter place he came under the influence of a powerful group of Southern writers known as the Nashville Agrarians, nicknamed the Fugitives from a magazine they edited. The Agrarians defended old-time Southern culture from what they thought was an insensitive modernist, industrialist attack. They stopped short of justifying secession and

---

47 Russell, *Edgar Lee Masters*, 277-79.

political independence, but they also had a deep void in their thought. They rarely considered the place of blacks in the American past, especially during the travail of slavery. It was so distracting. But they had great suspicion about the historical reputation of Abraham Lincoln. [48]

Mel Bradford would surpass them in defending secession, equal them in his lack of concern for blacks as slaves, and expand their attacks on Lincoln in a big way. Literary historians Frank Owsley, Robert Penn Warren, and Donald Davidson made the Agrarians' case against Lincoln as one of a lack of judgment and refusal to compromise. Unlike Bradford and Masters, they did not assail Lincoln's integrity. They would never have said, as did Bradford, with mock modesty, "The major charges [against Lincoln] advanced here, if proved, are sufficient to impeach the most famous and respected of

---

48 Clyde N. Wilson (ed.), *A Defender of Southern Conservatism: M. E. Bradford and His Achievements* (Columbia: University of Missouri Press, 1999), 9, 20, 43, 84, 91, especially the essay by Mark G. Malvasi, "All the Precious Things: M. E. Bradford and the Agrarian Tradition," 130-142. On the Agrarians, see Twelve Southerners., *I'll Take My Stand: The South and the Agrarian Tradition* (New York: Harper & Brothers, 1930). For Owsley, see Frank Owsley, "A Southerner's View of Abraham Lincoln," in Harriet C. Owsley (ed.), *The South: Old and New Frontiers* (Athens: University of Georgia Press, 1969), 223-35.

public men. More would only overdo."[49] Thus speaking,
"Bradford rode forth," in the words of one commentator,
"to lead is own intellectual Pickett's Charge against [the
president we all know best as] the Great Emancipator."[50]

Bradford saw Lincoln as a complicated man whose
public life went through three periods. The first was
the Whig phase, which stretched from his becoming
an adult until the passage of the Kansas-Nebraska Act.
This Lincoln was the economic man or "High Whig"
influenced by Henry Clay's American System. Here he
believed that law was law and scripture was scripture. But
he evidenced two disturbing qualities that will become
more important in later years, and, in Bradford's words,
"mark him as a dangerous man." These were his faith in
necessity and a feeling that he alone knew its disposition
for the future, both revealed in his 1838 "Springfield
Young Men's Lyceum Speech."

---

49 M. E. Bradford, "The Lincoln Legacy: A Long View," in
    his *Remembering Who We Are : Reflections of a Southern
    Conservative* (Athens: University of Georgia Press,1985),
    144. Many of Bradford's arguments were presaged in brief
    in Frank Meyer, "Lincoln Without Rhetoric," *National
    Review*, 17 (August 24, 1965, 725 and his "Lincoln
    Again," *ibid.*, 18 (January 25, 1966), 71, 85. See also,
    Thomas J. Pressly, "'Emancipating Slaves, Enslaving Free
    Men': Modern Libertarians Interpret the United States
    Civil War," *Civil War History*, 46 (No. 3, 2000), 254-65.
50 Wilson (ed.), *A Defender of Southern Conservatism*, 19.

The second period Bradford called the artificial Puritan years, from 1854 to Lincoln's accession to the presidency. Here Lincoln began to place more faith in necessity and spoke out on the slavery issue "wholly for effect." He showed a sense of his own destiny as the Caesar he spoke of in his Lyceum Address, who would gain absolute power by "*emancipating slaves or enslaving free men*." He had began to mix law with scripture.

Finally, there was the Cromwellian phase of the public Lincoln during the war itself, which Bradford called "the worst." The real is defined in terms of what is to come and only he understood what it was. He emancipated the slaves and enslaved the free, because God told him so. Lincoln's law was now scripture.[51]

Bradford assailed Lincoln's record as Cromwellian president in several areas, many of which echo Masters. He began by accusing Lincoln of "dishonesty and obfuscation" with respect to the African Americans, slave and free. This was a key ingredient to Lincoln's political success, Bradford said. Lincoln was able to appear "anti-

---

51 *Ibid.*, 143; and M. E. Bradford, "Dividing the House: The Gnosticism of Lincoln's Political Rhetoric," *Modern Age*, 23 (Winter 1979), 10-21, especially 20-21. The second stage of Lincoln's political development is detailed in Bradford, "Lincoln and the Language of hate and Fear: A Southern View," in his *Against the Barbarians and Other Reflections on Familiar Themes* (Columbia: University of Missouri Press, 1992), 229-45.

Southern or antislavery" without at the same time appearing to disparage the beginnings of the Republic, which was pro-Southern and pro-slavery. He moreover mastered this position without appearing pro-Negro. "He was the first Northern politician of any rank to combine these attitudes," according to Bradford.

Lincoln's political skill and "duplicitous rhetoric" on the African American's place in American society allowed him to combine and unite elements in the North that might ordinarily have been hostile, Bradford went on. It enabled him to compromise the Northern Democratic party by culling out its antislavery members and thus destroying the traditional national Democratic majority that had dominated American politics since the days of Thomas Jefferson. Lincoln insisted the black race was included in the Declaration of Independence ("all men are created equal"), but hinted that this need not apply to blacks in the North--or even in the South, after it had been morally purged of the "peculiar institution," as Southerners like to refer to slavery.

Under Lincoln, Bradford maintained, once the nation was freed from the blight of slavery, African Americans would experience "nothing more than a technical freedom" comprised of "empty words." Bradford accused Lincoln of leaving the nation with a "durable heritage of pious self-congratulation." America evidenced a "habit of concealing its larger objectives behind a façade of racial generosity, of using the Negro as a reason for policies and laws which make only minimal alterations in his condition; and also with the habit of seeming a great deal more than it is truly willing to give."[52]

Bradford's second accusation against the Lincoln record involved what he called "Lincoln's political economy," his management of the commercial and business life of North that later infected the whole nation as the "Great Barbecue," what Mark Twain cleverly labeled as the "Gilded Age," or what historian Mark W. Summers more cynically called the "Era of Good Stealings."[53] While many of the corruptions of the Republican Era came to

52 Bradford, "Lincoln Legacy," 144-46. See also, Bradford, "Dividing the House," 10-21, *passim*; and Bradford, "Commentary on 'Lincoln and the Economics of the American Dream'," in Gabor S. Boritt (ed.), *The Historian's Lincoln: Pseudohistory, Psychohistory, and History* (Urbana: University of Illinois Press, 1988), 107-123.

53 Samuel Langhorne Clemens [Mark Twain] and Charles Dudley Warner, *The Gilded Age* (Hartford: American Publishing Co., 1873); Mark W. Summers, *Era of Good Stealings* (New York: Oxford University Press, 1993). See also Summers other pieces, "'A Band of Brigands': Albany Lawmakers and Republican National Politics, 1860," *Civil War History*, 30 (1984), 101-19; *The Plundering Generation: Corruption and the Crisis of the Union* (New York: Oxford University Press, 1987); and *Railroads, Reconstruction, and the Gospel of Prosperity: Aid Under the Radical Republicans* (Princeton: Princeton University Press, 1984).

the fore after Lincoln's death, they began under Lincoln's direction or sponsorship, Bradford said, under the guise of "military necessity."

Basically, Bradford explained, creditors got the upper hand over debtors of the first time since Andrew Jackson destroyed the Second Bank of the United States. The government became the sponsor of a great transfer of wealth using the protective tariff on foreign imports (which rose from 18.84% in 1861 to 47.56% in 1865), the massive funding of internal improvements (especially the Pacific Railroad which led to the Crédit Mobilier scandal), a national banking system (that sponsored the creation of $480 million in fiat paper money to enhance credit for big business at the expense of small businesses and farms and later redeemed it one-to-one for gold), and the Homestead Act (in which less than 19% of the lands went to actual farmers, the rest to big businesses). "The Northern policy of importing immigrants with the promise of this land, only to force them into the ranks of General Grant's meatgrinder or into near slavery in the cities of the East," Bradford said, "requires little comment."

"From the beginning of the Republican Party Lincoln warned his associates not to talk about their views on these subjects," Bradford asserted. Lincoln blithely encouraged the" rotten army contracts system," "massive thefts of Southern property," allowing "special cronies and favorites of his friends to trade in Southern cotton," and a "calculated use of the patronage and the pork barrel" that resulted in "almost $10 million being pumped into local Republican organizations." All of this was accomplished on Lincoln's watch, Bradford concludes.[54]

But the corruption was not only economic, Bradford complains. Much of it was governmental, resulting in his "expansion of the powers of the presidency and his alteration of the basis for the Federal Union." Bradford asserts that Lincoln defined himself through his use of the presidential war powers. Bradford agrees with historian Clinton Rossiter that there were no logical limits to Lincoln's use of the war powers so long as he could use them in a holy cause. Others maintain that Lincoln acted much as the Committee of Public Safety during the French Revolution, except there were no executions on a massive scale. Since Lincoln's War of the Rebellion was an internal contest (among the states), it became an engine not only for defeating the Confederacy and preserving the Union. It also became "an instrument for transforming its nature," Bradford posits.

---

54 Bradford, "Lincoln Legacy," 146-49. See also the exchange between Bradford and Gabor S. Boritt, in Boritt (ed.), *The Historian's Lincoln: Pseudohistory, Psychohistory, and History*, 87-123.

Thus Lincoln became "our first imperial president" as "he summoned the militia, spent [unauthorized] millions, sanctioned recruiting, decreed a blockade, defied the Supreme Court, and pledged the nation's credit." He also established new units of government, appointed military officers to rule over the conquered sections of the South, seized property, arrested as many as 20,000 and put them in a Yankee "Gulag," closed over 300 newspapers, imported at least 500,000 foreign mercenaries (immigrants), and interfered in local elections in 1864 that garnered him a second term (when 38,000 votes might have changed the result). He also made a new state out of an old one using creative constitutional theories, dismissing it all as "expedient."[55]

Even more "expedient" and more damning in Bradford's eyes, was Lincoln role as military leader, which he defined as "commander and selector of Northern generals, chief commissary of Federal forces, and head of government in dealing with the leaders of an opposing power. In this role the image of Lincoln grows to very dark--indeed," Bradford whispers, "almost sinister." Basically, Bradford maintained that Lincoln did his best to keep the war going at all cost until he had achieved his domestic political purposes. He appointed Simon Cameron of Pennsylvania, a known corruptionist, as

---

55 Bradford, "Lincoln Legacy," 149-50.

Secretary of War, and kept similar hacks in power at lower levels and "winked at their activities," even after he had to fire Cameron as a sacrificial lamb.

"But all such mendacity was nothing in comparison to the price in blood paid for Lincoln's attempts to give the nation a genuine Republican [military] hero," Bradford argued. Until Generals U. S. Grant, W. T. Sherman, and P. H. Sheridan emerged late in the war, Yankee generals seemed to disapprove of Lincoln's policies or character. Lincoln threw many of the professionals (G. B. McClellan, FitzJohn Porter, W. B. Franklin, and D. C. Buell) to the Radical Republican wolves on the congressional Joint Committee on the Conduct of the War. Then he assigned "Republican" generals," champions of the 'new freedom,'" in Bradford's words, in their places (N. P. "Commissary" Banks [who supplied Confederate troops through his constant losses on the battlefields], B. F. "Beast" Butler [who looted Louisiana and the Gulf coast, while declaring New Orleans women who opposed him to be common prostitutes], J. C. Frémont [first Republican presidential candidate in 1865], John Pope [son of an old family friend], Franz Sigel [prominent German political leader], Lew Wallace [later author of *Ben Hur*], "Fightin' Joe" Hooker [who immodestly offered to become America's first military dictator], A. E. Burnside [who admitted to his inadequacies before he took command], and J. A.

McClernand [a loyal Democrat convert from Illinois]). Unfortunately, all of them stunk militarily.

"Thousands of Northern boys lost their lives in order that the Republican Party might experience rejuvenation, to serve its partisan goals," Bradford concluded. "All Lincoln asked of the ordinary Billy Yank was that he be prepared to give himself up to no real purpose--at least until Father Abraham found a general with proper moral and political credentials to lead him to Richmond," Bradford charged. Moreover, the heroes he found to lead his armies were the most vicious practitioners of war to date, laying the South to waste, presaging the horrible contests of the twentieth century. In 1864, as in 1861, Lincoln rejected out of hand all peace feelers from the Confederate side, regardless of terms. "He wanted total victory," Bradford asserts, "he needed a still-resisting, impenitent Confederacy to justify his re-election." Bradford blamed the deaths of over 100,000 Americans on Lincoln's refusing "an inexpedient peace."[56]

Next, Bradford charged Lincoln with causing the war in the first place, "the most serious of Lincoln's violations of the [p]residential responsibility." Lincoln well knew that his accession to office would produce a crisis of Union. But once secession took place, Lincoln expected to defeat it "swiftly with a combination of

---

56 *Ibid.,* 150-53.

persuasion, force, and Southern loyalty to the Union. The last of these," Bradford stated, "[Lincoln] completely overestimated." Bradford thought that Lincoln never expected "[a] full-scale Southern revolution, a revolution of all classes of [white] men against the way he and some of his supporters thought."

Bradford believed that Lincoln hoped for some small insurrection--something that he could use to unite the nation and stop secession cold. He needed a crisis, and to keep the United States Congress out of session, so that he could institute his new political order through executive fiat as war measures. "As he said to his friend, Senator Orville H. Browning of Illinois, 'The plan succeeded. They attacked Sumter--it fell, and thus did more service that it otherwise could.'" Lincoln also refused to publicize the South's offer to pay for Federal installations like Sumter, and to keep the Mississippi River open to commerce. It might have led to business as usual, compromise as in the past.

"Lincoln directed the nation away from the usual instinct to agree with the Constitution," Bradford said, to see law as a means to limit "government and the authority of temporary majorities, and of revisions in the law as the product of the ordinary push and pull within a pluralistic society, not as a response to the extralegal authority of some admirable abstraction like equality."

Indeed, Bradford was saddened that "[n]ot religion, but the cult of equality is the 'opiate of the masses' in today's world," that is, "a secular religion," and he warned that "most misery is caused by the pursuit of abstract happiness . . . ,"which can never be achieved.[57]

The fate of the nation "as left to us by Lincoln is that the Constitution is still to be defined by the latest wave of big ideas," Bradford said, "the most recent mass emotion." In the words of political scientist, Gottfried Dietz, whom Bradford quoted, Lincoln "opened the way for the development of an omnipresent president who as a spokesman for the people might consider himself entitled to do whatever he felt was good for the nation, irrespective of the interests and rights of the states, Congress, the judiciary, and the individual."[58]

---

57 M. E. Bradford, "On Remembering Who We Are," in his *Remembering Who We Are*, 11, 13; and *id.*, "Not So Democratic: The Caution of the Framers," in *ibid.*, 36. On the ideological unity of white, secessionist Southerners against Lincoln, see also, *id.*, "All To Do Over: The Secession of 1861," in *A Better Guide than Reason: Federalists and Anti-Federalists* (New Brunswick: Transaction Publishers, 1994), 153-167; and *id.*, "The Heresy of Equality: Bradford Replies to Jaffa," *Modern Age*, 20 (Winter 1976), 62-77.

58 Bradford, "Lincoln Legacy," 153-55. The final statement Bradford quotes from Gottfried Dietz, *America's Political Dilemma: From Lincoln to Unlimited Democracy* (Baltimore: The Johns Hopkins University Press, 1968), 58. For Bradford's strict construction of the Constitution,

Finally, Bradford found highly objectionable Lincoln's changing American political language to prevent future generations from reversing the ill effects of the trends he set in motion with his executive proclamations. Bradford called Lincoln "our first Puritan president." That is to say, Lincoln had the "habit of wrapping up his policy in the idiom of Holy Scripture, concealing within the Trojan horse of his gasconade and moral superiority an agenda that would never have been approved if presented in any other form."

That Lincoln was martyred only increased his moral authority, according to Bradford. "It is both unpatriotic and irreligious to look behind the words of so august a presence." Everything in American politics became "questions of ends[--]means are beside the point. And every 'good cause' is a reason for increasing the scope of government." Bradford concluded that Americans would be wise to recognize that under this political system, "[s]ome 'truths' are more important than the Truth. Even the Truth that we have a political tradition that is conservative and contrary to Lincoln."[59]

---

see Marshall L. DeRosa, "M. E. Bradford's Constitutional Theory: A Southern Reactionary's Affirmation of the Rule of Law," in Wilson (ed.), *A Defender of Southern Conservatism*, 92-129.

59 Bradford, "Lincoln Legacy,"155-56. See also, *id.*, "The Heresy of Equality: Bradford Replies to Jaffa," in *id.*, *A Better Guide than Reason*, 29-53, quote on 52. The tracing

Bradford's view of Abraham Lincoln reaped the critical whirlwind (especially after he compared Lincoln's sense of serving the Almighty to that of Adolph Hitler in a damnable footnote),[60] surpassing even Masters in its condemnation. He was astonished at the remarks, true and untrue, attributed to him in publications as diverse as the *New York Times, Washington Post, Los Angeles Times, New Republic, Chronicles of Higher Education, Wall Street Journal, Newsweek, the Keene [New Hampshire] Sentinel,* and the *CBS Evening New*s. He even figured in a Illinois congressional campaign, each candidate trying to out-do the other's jaundiced opinion of Bradford. The nicest comment on his viewpoint was the *Wall Street Journal's* calling his essays against Lincoln "terrible."

When he was nominated by President Ronald Reagan to head of the National Endowment for the Humanities, the explosions boomed out anew, causing him to be jettisoned for the less controversial (if that can

---

of Puritan influence from the English Civil War to the American Revolution to the American Civil War, without Master's or Bradford's censuring of Lincoln, is the theme of Kevin Phillips, *The Cousin's Wars: Religion, Politics, & the Triumph of Anglo-Americ*a (New York: Basic Books, 1999).

60 Bradford, "The Heresy of Equality," 56n36. In the same footnote, Bradford noted Edmund Wilson's comparing Lincoln to Otto von Bismarck and V. I. Lenin in *Patriotic Gore: Studies in the Literature of the American Civil War* (New York: Oxford University Press, 1962), xvi-xx.

be believed) William Bennett. Bradford commented on his notoriety thusly: "The myth of a 'second founding,' a 'new birth of freedom' among an 'almost chosen people,' embodies a heresy against the prescript of the [American] Revolution. And its hero-martyr-messiah is Abraham Lincoln . . . It is a powerful myth, able to threaten any and all who offend against it. . . ."[61] Bradford's refusal to go into the historical mist quietly confirmed the opinion of him once expressed by historian and Lincoln speech analyst Garry Wills, "suicidally frank."[62] Bradford gloried in this assessment until the day he died.

Bradford was not the only Lincoln critic to glory in his enemies. One of the more interesting attacks on Lincoln's reputation came from a noted black historian, social critic, and the current executive editor of *Ebony* magazine, Lerone Bennett, Jr. Educated at Morehouse College and Atlanta University, Bennett wrote of how "I was a child in whitest Mississippi, reading for my life, when I discovered that *everything* I had been told about Abraham Lincoln was a lie." Bennett was dismayed to learn "that I lived in an Orwelian world where scholars

---

61 Bradford, *Remembering Who We Are*, xvi-xvii.
62 Garry Wills, *Lincoln at Gettysburg: The Words that Remade America* (New York: Simon and Schuster, 1992), 39, as quoted in James McClellan, "Walking the Levee with Mel Bradford." In Wilson (ed.), *A Defender of Southern Conservatism*, 49.

with all degrees the schools give could say in all seriousness that a separatist was an integrationist and that a White supremacist was the ultimate symbol of race relations and the American Dream, . . [a man] whose deepest dream was a land without . . . African-Americans. . . ."[63]

As a magazine editor, Bennett approached his publisher with his views in the 1960s. John H. Johnson told him to write it, if he could prove it. The result was the controversial 1968 article, "Was Abe Lincoln a White Supremacist?"[64] Bennett was quickly condemned as a black radical militant. Noted Lincoln scholar, Herbert Mitgang, summed up the response of traditional historians in his essay, "Was Lincoln Just a Honkie?" where he suggested that for anyone to call Honest Abe a racist was racist in itself.[65]

Bennett examined further what he called "the abortive emancipation" during the "Great War between the Northern and Southern [White] Brothers" in a book length manuscript and found it even more wanting. Relying on already printed sources (both Masters and Bradford had covered much of the same ground),

63 Lerone Bennett, Jr., *Forced into Glory: Abraham Lincoln's White Dream* (Chicago: Johnson Publishing Company, 2000), viii, 147-48.

64 Lerone Bennett, Jr., "Was Lincoln a White Supremacist?" *Ebony*, 23 (1968), 35-38, 40, 42.

65 Herbert Mitgang, "Was Lincoln Just a Honkie?" *New York Times Magazine*, 11 (February 1968), 34-35, 100-107.

Bennett used what Lincoln and his defenders, then and now (whom he characterized as the "Abraham Lincoln Salvage Society"), wrote to show Lincoln as "a potentially great man flawed" by his own racist attitudes.[66] Bennett examined Lincoln from several perspectives, as a person, as a politician, as the Great Emancipator, and as an historical figure.

As a person, Bennett found Lincoln to be perpetually a poor Southern white from the day he was born until the day he died. But he was a man who had great ambition to rise above his class, Bennett said, which is revealed in Lincoln's passion for reading. It also was revealed in his Oedipal hatred of his father and all he represented as a subsistence farmer. Bennett believed that two events colored Lincoln's adult prejudices. One was the killing of his grandfather, also named Abraham, by Indians from ambush as he plowed his fields. This family hatred is what Bennett saw driving Lincoln's permitting the mass hanging of thirty-eight Santee Lakota at Mankato, Minnesota, for their war against white incursions on their land.

The other event that marked Lincoln's adult attitude concerned his taking a flatboat to New Orleans. Most remember this trip because he allegedly told his cousin Dennis Hanks that he was so appalled at the image of

---

66 Bennett, *Forced into Glory*, ix, 48, 140.

slavery that he would hit it hard if he ever got the chance. But the real occurrence of importance, Bennett said, was that the flatboat was attacked by black renegades near Baton Rouge and Lincoln and his companions barely escaped with their lives. Because of this and his poor white background, Bennett believed Lincoln always evidenced a fear of the black who was not enslaved or segregated and controlled in his economic, political, and sexual passions in competing against whites.[67]

Lincoln's politics revealed his ingrained distrust of blacks, Bennett said. Lincoln defined himself as a white man's politician. It was an integral part of his fundamental being. He gloried in telling racist jokes and dirty stories, and was close to a professional comedian as a politician could be. He used humor as a political weapon to identify with the crowd and deflect more serious issues. He especially loved jokes in dialect and quoted humorist Petroleum V. Nasby in cabinet meetings.

When friends told him that his stories were racist, cruel and even sadistic, Lincoln ignored them. It mitigated his cold, distant, strange moodiness. He called blacks niggers, darkies, boy, gal, auntie, uncle, to their faces without rancor, like any poor white of the time would. "[T]o say he was racist," Bennett asserted, "was to

---

67 *Ibid.*, 87-110, 155-65, 173-75, 254-58, 624. Ambition is a major theme in Fleming, "Lincoln's Tragic Heroism," 39-40.

understate the case. . . ," and Bennett disparaged modern historians who tried to label such accounts as false or just part of the times. Indeed, Bennett concluded, Lincoln's whole family, his political entourage, and his many friends were racist in talk, attitude, and jokes.[68]

Lincoln's politics were racist from the start, Bennett maintained. Contrary from his modern image, Lincoln was not a man of the people. In politics he was a High Whig. He believed in republican government of the best citizens, not democracy of the masses. Lincoln married into the Todd-Stuart-Edwards clique of Illinois politics, and he lusted after office like most men lust after women and money. He loved the view from the top and had no desire to slip back to his former station in life. When it appeared that several of his friends were implicated in the murder of Illinois abolitionist Elijah P. Lovejoy, Lincoln kept his mouth shut rather than risk his political career.[69]

Generally, Bennett said, Lincoln was a political chameleon of many colors, a fact brought out by his Democratic opponent, Stephen A. Douglas. In northern Illinois, according to Douglas, Lincoln was a "black abolitionist," in Egypt, he was a "white supremacist," and in middle Illinois, Lincoln was a "decent mulatto." He

---

68 Bennett, *Forced into Glory*, 13, 64, 85, 88, 96-97, 99-102, 107, 109, 198-99.

69 *Ibid.*, 68-73, 202, 215-18.

was against slavery in the abstract alone. In reality he was for leaving the institution be in the South, but he was for keeping it out of the territories, especially above the Missouri Compromise line. Beyond that, Bennett stated, Lincoln was as racist as Douglas, as their debates in the 1858 U.S. senator's race demonstrated. Indeed, between 1858 and 1860 Lincoln stated he was against equal rights for blacks at least twenty-one times, and for white supremacy eight times.[70]

The key to understanding Lincoln, Bennett maintained, was that, like his political mentor, Henry Clay, he was against slavery in the abstract. He rarely concerned himself with "real slavery or real Blacks. . . ." Lincoln was from Illinois, the state with the worst Black Code of any free state and many slave states, which Illinois toughened six times between statehood and the Civil War. None of that bothered Lincoln. He supported Illinois' Black Code and the Federal Fugitive Slave Act of 1850 (which Bennett characterized as the "Great American Slave Hunt") without protest, obeying the law like any World War II Nazi bureaucrat. He also introduced five emancipation decrees, two during the Civil War, one for the state of Delaware, and two while in Congress, all of which called for gradual, compensated abolition, with a long apprenticeship program and compulsory

---

70 *Ibid.*, 74, 219-27, 229-30, 305-34.

colonization abroad in Africa (Lincoln believed that all American slaves originally came from Liberia), Haiti (Isle la Vache) or Central America (where the colony would be named Lincolnia by a cynical press), or locally in Florida or Texas for all those freed.[71]

Paraphrasing Sandburg, Bennett declared that "Lincoln's Prairie Years were a perfect dress rehearsal for Lincoln's War Years, *on race.*" As his prior career had demonstrated, Bennett said, Lincoln had four basic principles when it came to race: keep blacks in slavery; if this failed, keep free blacks second class citizens; prevent racial amalgamation; preserve white supremacy. In the events leading up to the Emancipation Proclamation, Lincoln did not change his precepts on race, ever. Upon his election, Bennett claimed, Lincoln said to a friend, "I will be damned if I don't feel almost sorry for being elected when the niggers is the first thing I have to attend to."[72]

The first thing Lincoln did upon being elected president, Bennett continued, was to promise the South that his administration would not interfere with slavery where it existed, and backed a proposed constitutional amendment to that effect. He had his cabinet pledge to

---

71 *Ibid.,* 183-86, 188, 192-96, 197, 227, 233, 237-38, 241, 242, 244-45, 261, 267, 271-85, 286-97,381-87, 452-65, 527, 539, 546-47, 553-54.

72 *Ibid.,* 5, 79.

support the Fugitive Slave Act of 1850. Lincoln would not, however, compromise on Republican opposition to slavery in the territories, which Congress would end in June 1862. Even with the firing on Ft. Sumter, Lincoln stuck to his position that a rapid return of the South would preserve slavery as an institution. When individual army commanders (John C. Frémont in Missouri, David Hunter in South Carolina, Benjamin Butler in Virginia and Louisiana, John Phelps in Louisiana, and Simon Cameron as Secretary of War) tried to free the slaves in their command areas, Lincoln reprimanded, sacked, or demoted them.[73]

But with the Battle of First Manassas, Lincoln and the North belatedly learned that what Yankees derisively liked to call "Jeff Davis' Wheel Barrow Concern" had a chance to win the war. When the 37th Congress met on the 4th of July, Lincoln's strategy of avoiding slavery angered them. Congress then passed the two Confiscation Acts that permitted slaves to be seized, ended slavery in the District of Columbia and all territories (Lincoln waited two days before signing this to allow D.C. masters to escape into surrounding slave states with their chattels), changed the Articles of War to prevent the return of escaped slaves to their masters, set up the

---

73 *Ibid.*, 5, 13-14, 30-31, 246-54, 336, 337, 339, 340, 346-48, 358.

Joint Committee on the Conduct of the War to police the generals' politics, and recognized the black nations of Haiti and Liberia for the first time. Lincoln was fast becoming a man without a party.[74]

This was especially true when General George B. McClellan lost the Siege of Richmond and failed to crush General Robert E. Lee's army at Antietam. Lincoln had hoped that a McClellan victory would end the war, check Congress, and allow him to entice the South back into the Union leaving slavery intact. Now he had to act to slow the freedom process by introducing his preferred plan, the so-called Border State strategy of three constitutional amendments that would institute gradual emancipation with an apprenticeship period that would last until 1900, compensated emancipation for those slaves that were freed by accident during the war by coming into Union lines, and the forced colonization of all blacks beyond the borders of the United States. But when Lincoln tried to get the loyal slaveholders ("what a phrase," Bennett spat parenthetically) to approve of his strategy, they refused, even though Lincoln warned them, "[n]iggers will never be higher [in price]."[75]

So Abraham Lincoln introduced the Emancipation Proclamation. The Preliminary Proclamation was issued

74 *Ibid.,* 11-12, 371, 391-429, 430, 432, 433.
75 *Ibid.,* 6-12, 16, 26, 113, 354-57, 374-75, 414, 488 503, 509-12, 513-17.

September 22, as soon as the president determined that General McClellan was not going to destroy General Lee's Rebel army. Lincoln had no choice. Congress was threatening to withhold money for war supplies. The Second Confiscation Act had already called for the freeing of all slaves captured or fleeing to Union lines as contraband of war and would go into effect on September 23. In the Preliminary Proclamation Lincoln pledged that he would preserve slavery if the Confederates would come back into the Union within 100 days. If not, he would issue the Final Emancipation Proclamation which would free the slaves of all disloyal citizens still in the Confederacy. Meanwhile, he also had 100 days to get his three constitutional amendments through Congress.

Neither happened, so on New Year's Day 1863 Lincoln freed any slave in any jurisdiction he did not have control of. That is to say he freed no one, but those few who had been confiscated or fled slavery since the start of the war, estimated by Bennett, using figures supplied by Secretary of State Seward, as 200,000 by 1865. On the other hand, Bennett argues, the Emancipation Proclamation guaranteed the extended enslavement of nearly one million blacks who lived in the loyal Border States or occupied areas of the Confederacy exempt under the edict. Moreover, as a presidential decree of wartime necessity, Bennett pointed out, the Emancipation Proclamation was of doubtful legality.[76]

As Bennett saw it, the Emancipation Proclamation also had the traditional foreign policy element. It made it impossible for the European monarchies to openly assist and recognize the existence of the Confederate state. But if were not for the pressure from Congress and black and white abolitionists, Lincoln would have failed to act, even as half-heartedly as he did. Congress pressured him further by passing a law that freed the families of blacks, who enlisted in the Union army. Of course, enlistment granted freedom to the potential soldier on the spot. But many echoed the fear that emancipation by law or presidential fiat was illegal and unconstitutional. The result was, Bennett continued, Congress' refusal to adopt Lincoln's suggested three amendments and the substitution of a new Thirteenth Amendment for outright black freedom, passed by a congressional coalition cobbled together by Secretary of State Seward and ratified by the states, including the former Confederate states, as a part of President Andrew Johnson's Reconstruction

76 *Ibid.,* 6-8, 13, 17-20, 25-26, 434-35, 468, 497, 505-508, 537, 540-41. This figure is 10 times more than the one given in William C. Harris, "After the Emancipation Proclamation: Lincoln's Role in the Ending of Slavery," *North and South,* 42-53, although Seward's figure is from 1865 and Harris' is from 1863.

program on December 18, 1865. "Lincoln didn't make emancipation," Bennett contended, "emancipation, which he never understood or supported or approved, made Lincoln."[77]

If what Bennett said is true, how is it that Americans today do not know this? The answer, according to Bennett, is because of what he called the Lincolnologists, the largest army of mythologists ever mobilized to defend an American historical figure. ". . . Lincoln is theology," Bennett declared, "not historiology. He is a faith, he is a church, he is a religion, and he has his own priests and acolytes, most of whom have a vested interest in 'the great emancipator' and who are passionately opposed to anybody telling the truth about him. . . . He is also an industry. . . [Too many historians] earn a living feeding the Lincoln machine." Barbara Burns of the *New York Times* agreed with Bennett. "Lincoln is such a god that

---

77　Bennett, Forced into Glory, 8, 21, 58, 518-19, 534. A more conservative approach both praiseworthy and critical of Lincoln is William K. Klingaman, *Abraham Lincoln and the Road to Emancipation, 1861-1865* (New York: Viking, 2001. For a contrary interpretation favoring Lincoln's role in freeing the slaves, see Allen C. Guelzo, *Lincoln's Emancipation Proclamation: The End of Slavery in America* (New York: Simon & Schuster, 2004). On the Thirteenth Amendment, See Michael Vorenberg, *Final Freedom : The Civil War, the Abolition of Slavery, and the Thirteenth Amendment* (Cambridge ; New York : Cambridge University Press, 2001).

the rules of evidence do not apply to him." As satirical gadfly, cultural critic, and left-wing curmudgeon Dwight Macdonald once put it, "American literature is divided into three parts: fiction, nonfiction, and biographies of Abraham Lincoln."[78]

The facts about Lincoln are available to everyone, Bennett emphasized, why not examine them? The real problem is that they are deliberately overlooked, Bennett explained. It is a trained blindness--"generations of Lincoln scholars have been unable to see the N-word that can be found throughout the Lincoln record." Paul Angle once said reporters incompetently or incorrectly reported that Lincoln used such words, like nigger, darky, wench, buck, boy, gal, uncle, and auntie. But it was even worse, according to Bennett. After Lincoln's death, to honor him, many witnesses to his administration changed the record from the truth that happened.

Bennett called this process "post-assassination *reversus*," although the usual practice to cover this up was to dismiss Lincoln critics with adjectives like "extreme," or "shrill," or "hysterical." Lincoln supporters claim he was converted at the last moment before his tragic assassination and really did not mean all those horrible things he said about separation and deportation of freed persons--he just said them to get elected. "How," Bennett

---

78 Bennett, *Forced into Glory*, ix, 39, 51, 114.

asked, "to paraphrase the philosopher, do you hide the most celebrated man in American History? All ways are good, including Pulitzer Prizes and Memorials on the Mall."[79]

But "[i]f, despite the record, Lincoln has been misinterpreted," Bennett went on, "it is not his fault." Look at the various schools of history that surround his myth. "The dominant Lincoln school is the "See-No-Racism, Hear-No-Racism, Report-No-Racism School." But there is also the "Auteur School," in which the film director or historian substitutes a cardboard Lincoln for the real thing--before Lincoln speaks or acts they warn us that he really doesn't mean it. Then there is the "Isolated Quote School" which quotes Lincoln out of context to censor what we do not need to know. The "Feelgood School" employs the "Mother of All Lincoln Quotes" in which Lincoln reaches levels of eloquence unsurpassed by any other human being. The "Logos School" maintains that the Lincoln word is reality--in the beginning Lincoln was the word and the word was with Lincoln, and the word was Lincoln.

But there was more. "The Bogart School" in which Lincoln jukes his way along with unsupported assertions that turn facts and history upside down. One example is Gabor S. Boritt, who asserted that Lincoln made the

---

79 *Ibid.,* ix, 67, 97, 116, 117-19, 120, 143.

American dream the central idea of America, forgetting, according to Bennett, that Lincoln's only dream was for a white-only America of apartheid. The "Everybody Was a Racist School" maintains that Lincoln had to work within the system to get elected and could not sacrifice his career to just any silly statement supporting black suffrage. But Bennett wondered why there was never enough evidence that Lincoln *had* to say the racist things he did. Lots of other Americans of the time did not. Finally, there is "The Consent Theory of Government School," which holds that it would have been unjust to stop planters from enslaving blacks without giving slaveowners the right to vote on whether they wanted to give up their slaves. Its chief proponent, according to Bennett, is Harry V. Jaffa.[80]

There he is, then, the sixteenth president of the United States, according to Bennett. "Tragic and comic, humble and arrogant, sensitive and insensitive, humane, bigoted, superstitious, carrying the cross of Black fear and Indian fear and Woman fear, a man's man, never happier than when he was raising Cain with the boys on the circuit, and never completely comfortable in the presence of the ladies, lewd sometimes and often crude with the boys but eloquent on the stump, a White man's man who loved peace but volunteered three times to cleanse Illinois

---

80 *Ibid.*, 121-42.

of Indians, a lover of equality who told n[igge]r jokes, Pharoah and Moses, Macbeth and Minstrel, White on the outside and Black on the inside, a funny man and a sad one, always telling jokes on a high-wire above a personal abyss, trying to laugh away demons that repeatedly drove him to the edge of insanity, this is the Lincoln Nobody Wants to Know but the Lincoln Everybody Must Know if we are to understand the 'darkness' he feared and the whiteness that limited him."[81]

It was truly an ". . . irony of history," Bennett concluded, to "make an Illinois White supremacist the signer of the Emancipation Proclamation, . . . [and to] make a Virginia slaveholder the author of the Declaration of Independence, and with the same results." But we must choose what they really mean. "For by choosing our Lincoln--and our slavery--we choose our self, and our today." Bennett then added, "Lincoln is a key, perhaps the key, to the American personality and what we invest in him, and *hide* in him, is who we are." [82]

As columnist and editor Joseph Sobran declared, "Bennett's fury is entirely understandable and largely justified[, b]ut it leads him to excess." Moreover, he added, Bennett endorsed some of Lincoln's "worst deeds, such as his ruthless wartime measures and violations of

---

81 *Ibid.*, 85-86.
82 *Ibid.*, x, 59, 139.

the Constitution and civil liberties." It also led him to some historical errors. Bennett accused Lincoln as being as duplicitous with words as Booker T. Washington, yet Bennett himself parsed sentences with the skill of William J. Clinton when he said "slavery" is not mentioned in the Emancipation Proclamation. True, but "slave" is. "By selecting Lincoln's words carefully and placing his own interpretation on them," wrote Edward Steers, Jr., "Bennett is able to weave an ugly view of Abraham Lincoln that turns history on its ear. . . ."[83]

Most historians followed the lead of the late Jack Kemp, who wrote, "I take umbrage when the president known as the Great Emancipator is subjected to *ad hominem* attacks." Kemp pointed out Lincoln's statement in favor of blacks enjoying the natural rights embodied in the Declaration of Independence, which Bennett would dismiss as theoretical rather than actual. After all, the Declaration asserts that "all [white] men are created equal," according to Bennett. Like Bradford before him (although both would probably hate to be paired off in anything intellectual), Bennett was roundly condemned

---

83 Bennett, *Forced into Glory*, 16; Joseph Sobran, "Lincoln with Fangs," at http://sobran.com/columns/010208. shtml; Edward Steers, Jr., "Great Emancipator or Grand Wizard?" [Springfield Illinois] *State-Journal Register*, June 25, 2000.

for his efforts to make what historian Eric Foner called a "full-scale assault on Lincoln's reputation."[84]

Lincoln "richly deserves the credit for initiating and pushing forward under extraordinary circumstances the process by which this great republic would be free of its worse curse--chattel slavery," historian William C. Harris said. Edward Steers pointed out that Bennett's praise for the Second Confiscation Act as an emancipation document would have been contingent on individual court cases that could have lasted into the twentieth century. Michael Burkhimer noted that Lincoln's assassination revealed just how important emancipation was to him personally and how his increasing anti-slavery measures led to his death at the hands of openly avowed racists, who hated him for his actions against slavery. All of this led to black writer, Caesar A. Roy, to wonder if black Americans ought not to investigate Lincoln's public record more thoroughly and then join with black abolitionist Frederick Douglass in praising Lincoln's personal growth in office.[85]

---

84 Jack Kemp, "Assassins of Lincoln's Character Miss Their Mark," http://www.empoweramerica.org Reader$38 (May 16, 2001); Robert Stacy McCain, "Black Historian Documents Lincoln's Racism," *The Washington Times* (May 26, 2000), quoting Eric Foner.

85 Harris, "After the Emancipation Proclamation," 51; Steers, "Great Emancipator or Grand Wizard"; Caesar A. Roy, "Was Lincoln the Great Emancipator?" *Civil War Times Illustrated*, 33 (May/June 1994), 49.

Close on Bennett's heels came another book that looked at Lincoln in another way and once again found him lacking. Thomas DiLorenzo, an economist and historian, examined Lincoln's cleverly concealed economic agenda in his book, *The Real Lincoln*. Like those who preceded him, DiLorenzo agreed with Masters, Bradford and Bennett (although he fails to cite the latter two in his bibliography), differing only as to emphasis.

DiLorenzo began his attack on the Great Emancipator by examining Lincoln and the Lincoln Myth. Following Herndon's lead, DiLorenzo called Lincoln a master politician and an expert rhetorician, which meant he was a near genius of a wirepuller. DiLorenzo pointed out that Lincoln was the smartest parliamentarian and a most cunning logroller, a man who admired DeWitt Clinton, the former governor of New York. It was Clinton who introduced the spoils system into American politics, DiLorenzo noted, not Andrew Jackson. Then DiLorenzo quoted economist Murray Rothbard, "Lincoln was a master politician, which means that he was a consummate conniver, manipulator, and liar." This is why, DiLorenzo said, that ". . . one discovers that much of Lincoln historiography is not so much an attempt to explain history as to devise rationalizations or excuses for Lincoln's behavior."[86]

Next DiLorenzo challenged Lincoln's record on race. In this he repeated most of Bennett's arguments in less detail. DiLorenzo saw Lincoln as a typical white Northerner in his racial stereotypes. He was all for blacks not being slaves in theory, but stumbled when faced with the reality of blacks as free persons, denying them basic civil rights, and calling their removal from the United States as "glorious." DiLorenzo spent much time on Illinois' cruel Black Code, Lincoln's support of slavery in the South but not in the West, and noted that Alexis de Tocqueville mentioned that racial hatred was much more pronounced in free states than in the slave South. Before the war, blacks could vote only in Massachusetts, Vermont, New Hampshire and Maine, while they had had the vote removed from them in Connecticut and New Jersey. Few other states even considered allowing blacks to vote.[87]

Much of this nation-wide anti-Negro feeling came out in the aftermath of the Emancipation Proclamation, according to DiLorenzo. He asserted that 200,000 Northern white soldiers deserted in its aftermath;

---

86 Dilorenzo, *The Real Lincoln*, 10-11. For more on Rothbard, see Pressly, "'Emancipating Slaves, Enslaving Free Men'," 254-65.

87 Dilorenzo, *The Real Lincoln*, 3-4, 10-32.

120,000 more evaded conscription at home; and 90,000 fled to Canada to avoid any possibility of military service in Lincoln's Union. All this, despite that fact that the Emancipation Proclamation freed no slaves but those the Union forces could not touch. DiLorenzo claimed that the real purposes behind the Emancipation Proclamation was to keep European monarchies our of the war and to incite a slave rebellion to assist the floundering Union invasion of the South.[88]

But if Lincoln's approach to emancipation made his proclamation of January 1, 1863, "a gimmick," in the words of DiLorenzo supporter and fellow economist Walter Williams, DiLorenzo believed that the war and the emancipation that flowed from it had a more sinister purpose. And that goal explained why slavery in the United States had to be ended by violence rather than peacefully as in the rest of the Americas. Everywhere else the Industrial Revolution had destroyed slavery, a most inefficient type of labor ill-suited to the new order. But in the United States the Whig version of how to achieve industrialism had been voted down by the American people from the time of Jefferson and was seen as corrupt, a replication of the crooked English colonial approach

---

88 *Ibid.*, 4, 33-52, especially 45.

that had led to the American Revolution, and therefore unconstitutional.[89]

The reason that there had to be a war to end slavery in the United States was to guarantee the institution of Henry Clay's American System, Dilorenzo said, of which Lincoln was the prime proponent in 1860. Under the cover of saving the Union, Lincoln, by executive fiat, and the new Republican majority in both houses of Congress, could pass their economic system, so long blocked by Democrats, particularly from the South. Lincoln was always a High Whig, DiLorenzo contended, not a modern capitalist as historians Gabor S. Boritt and James M. McPherson said. Indeed, DiLorenzo claimed that Lincoln "seethed in frustration" at the lack of constitutional and popular support for the American system. Lincoln's plan was a mercantile ideology, a system which used faulty economic theory to build empires and subsidize individuals or groups or industries favored by the state. It was financed by a protective tariff which prevented free trade competition and raised local prices to consumers. It was a fancy cover for corporate welfare for select industries that ultimately led to empire--at first in

---

89　*Ibid.*, x, 38, 52-53, 83-84. See also, Walter Williams, "The Civil War Wasn't About Slavery," *Jewish World Review*, (December 2, 1998); "The Real Lincoln," *ibid.*, March 27, 2002; and "Secession or Nullification," at http://www.townhall.com/walterwilliams/ww20020410.shtml.

the American South and the Great West, and then in the 1890s, after these had been fully exploited, to American imperialism overseas.[90]

Because Southern Democats had been so long the central group around which opponents to the American System had coalesced, DiLorenzo said, it was imperative to keep the South out of the Union long enough to allow the Republican majority to enact its programs as war measures. By late 1862 or early 1863, Congress had enacted the American System in full with the new National Banking System and its paper money to inflate credit, the Pacific Railroad Act, and the Protective Tariff. Indeed, the tariff with its new rate of 80% was so central to Republican economic aspirations that DiLorenzo posited that secession was merely an extension of the old Nullification argument over the Tariff of Abominations of Andrew Jackson's day. And like in 1832, Lincoln expected that the South would come crawling back to the Union, in time.[91]

To justify the Republican war, Dilorenzo asserted that Lincoln had to get the South to fire the first shot to distract Northern opponents from the Republican economic program through a war-inspired patriotism for Union. This maneuvering and duplicity surrounding

90 Dilorenzo, *The Real Lincoln,* 3, 4-5, 54 84, 234.
91 *Ibid.,* 118-19, 121, 126, 128-29.

Ft. Sumter and Lincoln Administration relief efforts dovetailed with a Confederate objective--to get the rest of the slave South to secede and join the seven states already compromising the Confederacy. Here, both sides were half successful with four of the eight slave states left in the Union leaving over Lincoln's call for volunteers from all the states to quell what he and his cohorts called the War of the Rebellion. Lincoln also claimed secession to be illegal, following a dubious constitutional theory advanced (1832) and later repudiated (1850) by Daniel Webster, that the Union preceded the states in origin.

DiLorenzo called this "Lincoln's Spectacular Lie." He pointed out that there was no clause creating perpetual Union in the Constitution, that the states had declared independence and signed the Treaty of Paris in 1783 as separate entities, and that three states (Virginia, New York, and Rhode Island) had ratified the Constitution, reserving secession as a right that might be exercised later.[92]

Upon entering office, Lincoln effected many unconstitutional acts--the invasion of the South, the declaration of martial law, the creation of a naval blockade of Southern ports, the suspension of the writ of habeas corpus, the imprisonment of dissenters without trial, the shut down of critical newspapers, the

---

92 *Ibid.*, 5, 85-129.

censorship of telegraphic transmissions, the nationalizing of private railroads, the creation new states without the consent of the citizens of the states from which they came [the historically incorrect plural is DiLorenzo's], the interference in local elections by Federal troops, the deportation a member of Congress, the confiscation of private property and firearms, and the gutting of the Ninth and Tenth Amendments.

DiLorenzo was dismayed that Lincoln scholars find that these actions saved the Union by destroying much of the Constitution. Historians have long recognized Lincoln as dictator, DiLorenzo asserted, but usually they have tempered their notice by calling him a good or great one. The basic theme is that Lincoln's violation of the Constitution preserved it and those who disagree are dismissed as "extremists." DiLorenzo marveled that Lincoln defender Clinton Rossiter could write a book entitled *Constitutional Dictatorship*, without realizing what a contradiction in terms that implied. The wartime Republicans were not so smug. Congress passed an indemnity act to declare all presidential, cabinet, and military actions valid in 1863. The measure passed the House of Representatives but not the Senate. The presiding officer of the Senate was up to the task--he simply declared it passed. [93]

---

93 *Ibid.,* 5-6, 130-69.

As the action of Congress demonstrated, DiLorenzo maintained, Lincoln abandoned the accepted international rules of war, which had just been codified in Geneva in 1863, and micro-managed the war effort himself. Lincoln initiated his own code of war, the Lieber Code, which had an important exemption clause at the end that permitted military commanders to ignore it if necessary. Federal armies practiced rampant vandalism without any Lincoln rebuke, DiLorenzo said. Lincoln had the South punished for its intransigence by burning out towns and sacking plantations.

DiLorenzo noted that Lincoln used deadly force against anyone in favor of secession, military or civilian. The arrest and hanging of 39 of 303 Santee Lakota with the pledge the rest would be deported out of the state, and the exile of entire civilian populations out of western Missouri to try and end guerrilla depredations were examples. This was an intentional Lincoln policy, DiLorenzo asserted, and the generals like Pope, Grant, Sherman, and Sheridan merely carried it out. DiLorenzo also charged that there was much rape in Sherman's march across Georgia and South Carolina, especially against black women.[94]

DiLorenzo attributed three historical legacies to Lincoln's conduct during the Civil War, two short term

----

94　*Ibid.*, 6-7, 171-99.

and one long term. The first was a political outcome called Reconstruction, in which the defeated South was plundered primarily through new, Republican higher taxes and railroad schemes. The government of the nation was further consolidated in Washington, D.C., and the military supervised Southern elections until the final corrupt political outburst in 1876 and 1877. Included in this Yankee imperial conquest was the crushing of the Plains Indians out West.

DiLorenzo found that the fact the Federal government felt it necessary for the South to repudiate secession and ratify the Thirteenth, Fourteenth, and Fifteenth Amendments gave lie to Lincoln's assertions that leaving the Union was illegal. Moreover, the new amendments forced the black vote on both North and South because one of the curious results of Confederate defeat was that the South received more congressmen after 1865. Now all blacks were counted toward representation, not just three-fifths as under slavery. The new amendments also stopped the anti-Negro civil rights foot-draggers among the old free states, and provided the Republican electoral edge until 1932, with the exceptions of Woodrow Wilson (who would not have won in 1912 had the Republicans not split between Taft and Teddy Roosevelt, nor in 1916 had not World War I been an issue) and Grover Cleveland (who was as big a Gold Bug as his Republican opponents, James G. Blaine and Benjamin Harrison).[95]

The second legacy of the Civil War was the Gilded Age. It was not that government had not been corrupt before. But now the centralizing of political power in Washington made everything more potent and complete, just as Thomas Jefferson and Martin Van Buren through his front man Andrew Jackson had feared. Leading the way in corruption were the railroads which looted the public treasury through subsidies that included most of the vacant land up for homesteading. DiLorenzo used the example of James J. Hill's Great Northern Railroad, financed privately, to show that another alternative to public corruption existed.[96]

Finally, DiLorenzo said, the Lincoln prosecution of the war had the long-term legacy of destroying the notion that the nation was a voluntary association of states which had existed from the time of the Founding Fathers. The war destroyed the concept of state rights and secession to check the power of the federal government, which had been advocated by Thomas Jefferson and James Madison to attack the Alien and Sedition Acts in 1798; by the Hartford Convention to protest the War of 1812 in 1814; and by South Carolina to nullify the Tariff

---

95 *Ibid.*, 7, 200-32.
96 *Ibid.*, 7-8, 233-56.

in 1832. The Republicans preferred the Federalist Party solution advanced by Chief Justice John Marshall, that the U.S. Supreme Court would reserve this state-asserted nullification function to itself in a case by case manner. Lincoln saved the Union by increasing the central political control coming out of Washington and destroying the Ninth Amendment (which guarded against government intrusion upon personal liberty) and Tenth Amendment (which reserved all powers not specifically granted to the federal government to states and the people) through the Fourteenth Amendment (which limited state rights and ultimately, through judicial review, instituted the Bill of Rights, originally designed to limit the federal government, against the States)

As John C. Calhoun had written, the essential question of American politics was "whether ours was a federal or consolidated government; a constitutional or absolute one; a government resting solidly on the basis of the sovereignty of the States, or on the unrestrained will of a majority; a form of government, as in all unlimited ones, in which injustice, violence, and force must ultimately prevail." DiLorenzo put it a little differently: Lincoln had let the genie of centralism out of the bottle never to be returned, as successive administrations, Republican or

Democrat, have shown. Ending slavery was a by-product designed to cover the real Republican program.[97]

DiLorenzo's *Real Lincoln* brought the ideologues of every brand out of the woodwork. Critics charged that DiLorenzo's account was a "rehash of Confederate propaganda," and "had its antecedents in Southern editorials during and after the Civil War" (leading one to wonder why is it supporters of Lincoln never rehash Yankee propaganda and Northern editorials). DiLorenzo's notion that slavery could have been ended peacefully ignored the fact that the South felt otherwise. Even loyal slave states refused to consider compensated emancipation. DiLorenzo's emphasis on the economic causes of the war were as old as Charles and Mary Beard and numerous neo-Marxist interpretations of American history from the 1930s. "*The Real Lincoln* constitutes little more than a raid on history," concluded one avowed Lincolnite.[98]

But unlike previous volumes, DiLorenzo's stirred up a rousing defense. The debate on Lincoln as president became a political debate of the current state of American government. Many Conservatives, Neo-Conservatives, and Libertarians, had been ambivalent about Lincoln for

---

97 *Ibid.,* ix, xi, xii, 2, 8-9, 122, 257-79.

98 Mackubin Thomas Owens, "Real Lincoln Not Found in Book," *Washington Times*, May 4, 2002.

some time.[99] Now the reasons why came hot and heavy, leading to as much name-calling as scholarly debate. Proponents of DiLorenzo's thesis that Lincoln destroyed constitutional government and ushered in the age of big government, big business corporate welfare, spendthrift and corrupt congresses, total war, ethnic cleansing, and violent nationalism and internationalism were condemned by Lincolnites who called their antagonists advocates of White Citizens Councils, disingenuous supporters of Jim Crow (or segregation of the races), sloppy scholars, downright liars, sophomoric, and fundamentally wrong-headed in their notions of what North and South stood for during the Civil War era. "Of course, there are genuine criticisms, and then there are smears," remarked one DiLorenzo advocate, dryly.[100]

---

99 See Pressly, "'Emancipating Slaves, Enslaving Free Men'," 254-65.

100 Some sixty articles and links from both sides in this argument *ad nauseam*, may be found in "The King Lincoln Archive," at http://www.lewrockwell.com/orig2/lincoln-arch.html. Quote from David Dieteman, "Unpleasant Truths," *ibid.* See also, Jack Kemp, "Assassins of Lincoln's Character Miss Their Mark," http://www.empoweramerica.orgReader$38 (May 16, 2001); Harry V. Jaffa, "*In Re* Jack Kemp v. Joe Sobran on Lincoln," and Seth Leibsohn, "Lincoln and life: An Observation on the Kemp-Sobran-Jaffa Debate," at http://www.Claremont.org/old/publications/jaffa010730.cfm, and leibsohn010807.cfm; Joseph Sobran, "The Imaginary Abe: A Reply to Harry Jaffa . . . ," at http://www. Sobran.

From the halls of not-too-staid academia, like the famous Claremont Institute, the debate went public. Geoff Metcalf of World News Daily had both sides going on the radio and the internet. Noted Liberal-basher Rush Limbaugh introduced his misgivings about DiLorenzo's Lincoln to his radio audience, expecting widespread agreement, only to find that his usually devoted Dittoheads were latent Northern and Southern secessionists, suddenly turned verbally violent and, in the words of one observer, fast "Flunking Out of the Limbaugh Institute" for Advanced Conservative Studies. [101]

com/replyjeffa.shtml; Thomas J. DiLorenzo, "Lincoln's Tariff War," and Staff, "Confronting the Lincoln Cult: An Interview with Thomas DiLorenzo," at http://www. mises.org/fullstory.asp?control=952&FS=Lincoln%27s% 2Btarriff%2 Bwar, and 973&FS=Confronting%2Blinco ln%2Bcult#top; Tibor R. Machan. "Lincoln, Secession, and Slavery," at http://cato.org/cgi-bin/scripts/printtech. cgi/dailys/06-01-02.html; Jude Wanniski, "Defending Abraham Lincoln," and "Lincoln on the Fourth of July, 1861," at http://www.twonhall.com/columnists/ judewanniski/jw20020625.shtml, and jw20020706. shtml; Ilana Mercer, "Lincoln's Legacy of Corruption," Thomas J. Lorenzo, "Let the *Ad Hominem* Begin," and his "More *Ad Hominem*," and David Quackenbush, "Examining 'Evidence' of Lincoln's Tyranny," at http:// www.wnd.comnews/printer-friendly/.asp? ARTICLE_ ID=26440, and 26539, 26610, and 27346.

101 Geoff Metcalf, "Lincoln: Tyrant or Champion... Or Both?" at http://www.wnd.com/news.article.asp?ARTICLE_ ID=27512, and 27255, and 27396; Ken Masugi.

Left out in all this discussion was the notion that modern American Liberalism in all its aspects including big government and the nanny state, actually began during the Progressive movement, somewhere between the presidencies of Theodore Roosevelt and his cousin Franklin. "Big Government began when Woodrow Wilson and Herbert Croly rejected Lincoln's (and Taft's, and Coolidge's) Republicanism," said one reviewer of DiLorenzo's *Real Lincoln*, "because they discerned at its heart the founders' republicanism."[102]

What are we to make of all this? Historian Thomas Fleming has suggested that there is "no doubt of Lincoln's greatness. He is our Julius Caesar, our Cromwell; and our estimation of his services depends a great deal on our views of the other great men who have fought civil wars and reconstructed nations."[103] More important, the critics

---

"Flunking Out of the Limbaugh Institute," at http://www.claremont.org/old/precepts/267.cfm.

102 Charles R. Kesler, "Getting Right with Lincoln: Why Lincoln's Conservative Critics Are Wrong," at http://national review,com/dissent/dissentprint022101.html. For a critique of Kesler, see Myles Kantor, "Charles Kesler's Lincolnitis," at http://www.lewrockwell.com/kantor/kantor2.html.

103 Fleming, "Lincoln's Tragic Heroism," 39-40. The caesarian imperial theme is central to Greg Loren Durand, *America's Caesar: Abraham Lincoln and the Birth of a Modern Empire* (3rd ed., 2001) at http://www.crownrights.com/caesar, who maintains, moreover, that the United States has been under martial law at least since march 1933.

of Lincoln as president might have a few of the answers as to what made John Wilkes Booth and his many co-conspirators tick.

If it is true that Lincoln achieved apotheosis only after his death, it is quite possible that the man who killed Lincoln killed a different being than now exists in our history and legend.[104] This means that, unlike now, one hundred and fifty years after the fact, when serious scholars are calling for re-thinking what the Constitution means in light of its allegedly imperfect democratic nature as revealed by the Civil War (so much for the Founding fathers' republican government),[105] Lincoln's election and governing were quite a shock to the prewar American political mind, especially that in the slave South.

It means that John Wilkes Booth was not crazy, but quite possibly more sane than modern Americans are willing to accept—that the "Crime of the Century" was nothing more than, in the cynical words of anti-fascist

104 Most instructive of the Lincoln Booth and his contemporaries knew is Larry Tagg, *The Unpopular Lincoln: The Story of America's Most Reviled President* (El Dorado Hills, Calif.: Savas Beatie, 2009).

105 See, *e.g.*, Walter Williams, "Are We a Republic or a Democracy?" at townhall.com, January 5, 2005; Robert A. Dahl, *How Democratic Is the American Constitution?* (New Haven: Yale University Press, 2002), and the even more provocative review by Hendrik Hertzberg, "Framed Up: What the Constitution Gets Wrong," *The New Yorker*, 78 (July 29, 2002), 85-90.

poet and chronicler of the Spanish Civil War, W. H. Auden, a "necessary murder." Booth was simply a day late and a dollar short in his response to the threat that faced the Constitution and Union. But the Confederacy was like that.

Another more recent commentator, American Enterprise Institute think tank member Michael Ledeen, put it like this: "I always thought that John C. Calhoun was right about secession . . . and Lincoln was wrong. But I'm glad Lincoln was wrong, and won."

But conservative commentator, Jonah Goldberg, tried another approach. He conducted an informal poll that garnered over 1600 responses on the question of "Abe Lincoln, Tyrant or hero?" The response was unexpected in its volume, admitted Goldberg. He went on, somewhat tongue-in-cheek, "[I]t generates too much e-mail and my lips are pretty tired from reading it all. . . .Besides," Goldberg asserted," I think this is about right. He was 86% hero and 14% tyrant."

Such attitudes long ago caused a disgusted Fugitive poet and Southern historian, Alan Tate, to have a fictional Confederate veteran lament in his literary piece about the loss of the War for Southern Independence, thusly: "[Now, we a]ll are born Yankees of the race of men."[106]

---

106 Jonah Goldberg, "Abe's End," at http://www.nationalreview. com/goldberg032399.html; Michael Ledeen in "A Critical Look at Lincoln: Was the 16th a Saint or a Devil?

In other words, Tate would maintain, in the manner of George Lucas, that the republic morphed into the empire and Anakin Skywalker became Darth Vader. But as loyal imperial citizens, observers, and historians--unlike John Wilkes Booth--we dare not see it.

A Symposium," at http://www. nationalreview.com/ weekend/presidents/presidents-symposiumprint021701. html; Allen Tate, *Collected Poems, 1919-1976* (New York: Farrar Straus Giroux, 1977), "To the Lacedemonians [an old name for Spartans]," 85-88.

II.

Out of the Sahara of the Bozart: The Pre-War Political Thought of John Wilkes Booth

It has never been easy being a white Southerner. Ask any Yankee. "[White Southerners] seldom show any spirit of enterprise, or expose themselves willingly to fatigue," opined one pre-Civil War Northern critic. They are ignorant and "delight in their present low, lazy, sluttish, heathenish, hellish [l]ife, and seem not desirous of changing it," agreed another.

"Here is the grand distinction between [the white Southerner] and the Northerner," said landscape architect Frederick Law Olmstead, designer of New York's Central Park and mid-nineteenth century traveler of the South and commentator on its lifestyle. "[T]he Northerner . . . finds his happiness in doing. Rest, in itself, [unlike to the white Southerner], is irksome and offensive to him."[1]

---

1 Various quotes from Forrest McDonald and Grady McWhiney, "The South from Self-sufficiency to Peonage: An Interpretation," *American Historical Review*, 85 (December 1980), 1095-1118, especially at 1095. For Olmsted, see Frederick Law Olmstead, *A Journey in the Seaboard Slave States, with Remarks on their Economy* (New

Disparagement of the white South is a Northern hobby that has not stopped with the Civil War. According to noted modern-day Southern scholar Dewey Grantham, "[n]on-Southerners have been long accustomed to thinking of the southern region as separate from the rest of the country, as aberrant in attitude and defiant in mood, and as differentiated in some mysterious way from the national experience and the national ideas. . . . There is, moreover, an exotic quality about the South," Grantham continued, "and its mystery and mystique make it in [historian] David Potter's words, 'a kind of Sphinx on the American land.'"[2]

"I'll tell you why [that is so]," groused Georgian Matt Towery, recently. "It's because know-it-alls in New York

---

York: Dix and Edwards, 1856), *A Journey in Texas; or, a Saddle-trip on the Southwestern Frontier: with a Statistical Appendix* (New York: Mason Bros.,1857), *and a Journey in the Back Country: Our Slave States* (New York: Mason Bros., 1861), which have been abridged and edited in Olmstead, *The Cotton Kingdom: A Traveler's Observations on Cotton and Slavery in the American Slave States* (New York: Da Capo Pr, 1986). See also, Lee Hall, *Olmsted's America: An "Unpractical" Man and His Vision of Civilization* (Boston: Bulfinch Press, 1995); Laura Wood Roper, *FLO: A Biography of Frederick Law Olmsted.* (Baltimore: Johns Hopkins University Press, 1973).

2   Dewey Grantham, Jr. (ed.), *The South and the Sectional Image: The Sectional Theme since Reconstruction* (New York: Harper & Row, 1967), 2; David Potter, "The Enigma of the South," *Yale Review*, 51 (October 1961), 142.

and Washington don't have a clue about the American South. . . . They assume we are dumb and poorly educated."[3]

Yet no Northerner has ever unmasked the Sphinx of the South more thoroughly and acerbically than did a native scion, the resident literary curmudgeon of *The Baltimore Sun*, H.L. Mencken, in his classic essay, "The Sahara of the Bozart," which was first published in 1917, just before the dawn of the 20th century Southern intellectual renaissance.[4] Of course, Mencken's "Bozart" (that's spelled "b-e-a-u-x-a-r-t-e-s," in more sophisticated, frenchified circles) were the fine arts, of which he maintained the South, "that gargantuan paradise of the fourth-rate," as he put it, had none.

"Down there a poet is now almost as rare as an oboe-player, a dry-point etcher, or a metaphysician," he claimed. The South has "[n]o critics, musical composers, painters, sculptors, architects and the like, . . . not even

---

3   Matt Towery, "The Elite Doesn't Understand the South," at www.townhall.com/columnists/matttowery/mt2005090. shtml (Sept. 1, 2005).

4   This and all succeeding quotes from H. L. Mencken, "The Sahara of the Bozart," *New York Evening Mail* of November 13, 1917. For the intellectual environment "Bozart" appeared in, consult Fred Hobson, *Serpent in Eden: H.L. Mencken and the South* (Baton Rouge: Louisiana State University Press, 1974), 11-32. Another version of "Bozart" appeared in Mencken's *Prejudices. Second Series* (New York: A.A. Knopf, 1920), 136-54.

a bad one between the Potomac mud-flats and the Gulf. Nor an historian. Nor a philosopher. Nor a theologian. Nor a scientist. In all these fields the South is an awe-inspiring blank," Mencken asserted.

It is, indeed, amazing, he continued, "to contemplate so vast a vacuity." The South, Mencken concluded, "is almost as sterile, artistically, intellectually, [and] culturally, as the Sahara Desert."

It did not take long before, in the words of one supporter, "a lynching party awaited H.L. Mencken at all points south of Maryland," which, of course, merely proved his point.[5] Unfortunately, modern, proto-Abolitionist scholars, who should know better, have too easily fallen into Mencken's hyperbolic trap of the "intellectual . . . Lapland" of the South, when it comes to examining the political thought of John Wilkes Booth, the notorious (in their eyes, at least) assassin of Abraham Lincoln.

These allegedly politically correct historians believe that Booth, like Mencken's quintessential Southern male, simply could not think for himself. Somehow, Booth was mentally deficient. His sexual excesses, hard drinking,

---

5   Hobson, *Serpent in Eden*, 28 (Quoting Southern poet James Branch Cabell).

and inability to get along with those of authority starkly revealed his emotional immaturity.[6]

Indeed, Booth's historically recorded quirks are a veritable psychologist's dream. According to the analysts, Booth killed the president because Lincoln allegedly represented an absentee father, whom Booth hated for his illegitimacy;[7] or because Booth had a deep-seated Oedipal urge to impress a mother, who spoiled him incessantly;[8] or because Booth had a need to rise above

6   Jim Bishop, *The Day Lincoln Was Shot* (New York: Harper Brothers, 1955), 297; Charles E. Holding, "John Wilkes Booth in Nashville," *Tennessee Historical Quarterly*, 73-79, and John S. Kendall, *The Golden Age of the New Orleans Theater* (Baton Rouge: Louisiana State University Press, 1952), 497, accuse Booth of being drunk while acting on stage; James McKinley, *Assassination in America* (New York: Harper & Row, 1977), 28; Edward Hyams, *Killing No Murder: A Study of Assassination as a Political Means* (London: Thomas Nelson and Sons, Ltd., 1969), 68, 83; James W. Clarke, *American Assassins: The Darker Side of Politics* (Princeton: Princeton University Press, 1982), 18-19. The most complete study of the various theories as to why Booth killed Lincoln is William Hanchett, *The Lincoln Murder Conspiracies* (Urbana: University of Illinois Press, 1983).

7   George W. Wilson, "John Wilkes Booth: Father Murder," *American Imago*, 1 (1940), 49-60.

8   Barbara Lerner, "The Killer Narcissists," *National Review On-line*, May 19, 1999, at townhall.com.

his older brothers, who were arguably better actors than he. The litany goes on and on.[9]

Even if Booth were given credit for organizing his own compact murder conspiracy, he suffered. Instead of being a *bona fide* Confederate hero, as he thought of himself, he became the victim of an "outmoded feudal culture" caught up in regional warfare, which caused him to act the part of executioner as "misguided or deluded hero," the reincarnation of the Roman murderer of Julius Caesar, Marcus Brutus--but an "American Brutus," a character borrowed and internalized from the Shakespearean plays he so loved.[10]

Booth was too easily dismissed as a "vulgar cut-throat," leading a "Gang of Cartoon Assassins" in a morbid thirst for notoriety, seeking revenge against Lincoln for hanging Confederate spy and *agent provocateur*, John Yates Beall (a supposed Booth friend).[11] Or was he more

---

9   Philip Weissman, "Why Booth Killed Lincoln: A Psychoanalytic Study," *Psychoanalysis and the Social Sciences*, 5 (1958), 99-115.

10 Michael Kauffman, *American Brutus: John Wilkes Booth and the Lincoln Assassination* (New York: Random House, 2004); Diana L. Rubino, *A Necessary End* (Stardustpress. com, 2007); Timothy Crouse, "A Conspiracy Theory to End All Conspiracy Theories: Did John Wilkes Booth Act Alone?" *Rolling Stone*, 216 (July 1, 1976), 42-44, 47, 91-92, 94.

11 Isaac Markens, "President Lincoln and the Case of John Yates Beall," http://www.geocities.com/Athens/5568/jyb.

a "frustrated ham actor" losing his stage voice because of poor speaking technique, deathly ill and out of his mind from raging syphilis, an egotist fearful of "becoming a nobody," who now had to make a splash in a field other than the theater?[12]

---

html. See also, William A. Tidwell, "John Wilkes Booth and John Yates Beall," *Surratt Courier*, 25 (November 2000), 3-5; and J. Ninian Beall, "Why Booth Killed Lincoln," Columbia Historical Society of Washington, D.C., *Records*, 48-49 [1946-47], 127-41.

12 More general materials from the preceding three paragraphs are from Hanchett, *The Lincoln Murder Conspiracies*, 35-58; Constance Head, "John Wilkes Booth as Hero Figure," *Journal of American Culture*, 5 Fall 1982), 22-28; Philip Van Doren Stern, *The Man Who Killed Lincoln: The Story of John Wilkes Booth and His Part in the Assassination* (New York: The Literary Guild of America, 1939) (outmoded); James McKinley, *Assassination in America* (New York: Harper & Row, 1977), 10 (misguided or deluded hero), 28; Kauffman, *American Brutus*; Francis Wilson, *John Wilkes Booth: Fact and Fiction of Lincoln's Assassination* (Boston: Houghton Mifflin Co., 1929), ix-x (vulgar, notoriety); Lloyd Lewis, *The Assassination of Lincoln: History and Myth* (Lincoln, Neb.: Bison Books, 1994, orig., 1929), 158-74 (cartoon assassinations); Larry Starkey, *Wilkes Booth Came to Washington* (New York: Random House, 1976) (Beall); James W. Clarke, *American Assassins*, 18-19 (ham actor); Stanley Kimmel, *The Mad Booths of Maryland* (2nd ed., rev. and enlarged, New York: Dover Publications, 1969), 262 (Booth's voice, fear of becoming a nobody). The quarrel over Booth's possibly having syphilis is in David Dillon (ed.), *The Lincoln Assassination: From the Pages of the Surratt Courier* (13 parts, Clinton, Md : The Surratt Society, 2000), XIII, 7-14. The chronic hoarseness and

Many others preferred to see Booth a mere, thoughtless, racist cog in the wheel of a vast conspiracy thought out by others, almost too numerous to mention. These included the leaders of the Confederacy, bent on revenge for Lincoln's bloody, tyrannous victory in the Civil War;[13] or the independently-organized Knights of the Golden Circle, who envisioned the continuation of a Southern slave empire in soon-to-be-conquered lands around the periphery of the Caribbean Sea and the Gulf of Mexico.[14]

---

sore throat could have come from a ill-advised winter journey across Missouri in the snow during the dead of winter, rather than poor voice projection, see Rhodehamel and Taper (eds.), *Writings of John Wilkes Booth*, 97-98n.5.

13 Hanchett, *The Lincoln Murder Conspiracies*, 59-89; Benn Pittman (comp.), *The Assassination of President Lincoln and the Trial of the Conspirators* (Cincinnati: Moore, Wilstach & Baldwin, 1865), particularly the testimony of Charles Dunham, Richard Montgomery and Dr. James B. Merritt; Francis Wilson, *John Wilkes Booth: Fact and Fiction of Lincoln's Assassination* (Boston: Houghton Mifflin Co., 1929), ix-x ; Starkey, *Wilkes Booth Came to Washington*; William A. Tidwell, James O. Hall, and David Winfred Gaddy, *Come Retribution: The Confederate Secret Service and the Assassination of Lincoln* (Jackson: University Press of Mississippi, 1988).

14 Izola Forrester, *This One Mad Act . . . : The Unknown Story of John Wilkes Booth and His Family* (Boston: Hale, Cushman, & Flint, 1937), vii. On the Knights of the Golden Circle and Southern filibustering expeditions, consult Robert E. May, *The Southern Dream of a Caribbean Empire, 1854-1861* (Baton Rouge: Louisiana State

But there is more. Some assert that Booth was a pawn in anti-Lincoln schemes involving Northern Radical Republican politicians and Union executive department officials, disgruntled at Lincoln's allegedly soft treatment of the surrendering Rebels, or out for unmentioned personal gain, most often involving shady schemes to cash in on the international cotton market or various forms of illicit trade with the Confederacy;[15] or certain of Lincoln's own cabinet, again angling for a harsh Reconstruction of

---

University Press, 1973), 3, 20, 49, 91-94, 148-55; Olliger Crenshaw, "The Knights of the Golden Circle," *American Historical Review*, 47 (1941), 23-50; C. A. Bridges, "The Knights of the Golden Circle: A Filibustering Fantasy," *Southwestern Historical Quarterly*, 287-302; Joe A. Stout, Jr., *The Liberators: Filibustering Expeditions into Mexico, 1848-1862, and the Last Gasp of Manifest Destiny* (Los Angeles: Westernlore Press, 1973), and Stout, *Schemers and Dreamers: Filibustering in Mexico, 1848-1862* (Ft. Worth: Texas Christian University, 2002. Both Booth and neighbor T. William O'Laughlen (if not his brother Mike, too, later a co-conspirator against Lincoln) were rumored to be members of the Golden Circle. See also, Warren Getler and Bob Brewer, *Shadow of the Sentinel: One Man's Quest to Find the Hidden Treasure of the Confederacy* (New York: Simon and Schuster, 2003).

15 See Charles Higham, *Murdering Mr. Lincoln: A New Detection of the 19th century's Most Famous Crime* (Beverly Hills: New Millennium Press, 2004); and Leonard F. Guttridge and Ray A. Neff, *Dark Union: the Secret Web of Profiteers, Politicians, and Booth Conspirators that Led to Lincoln's Death* (Hoboken, N.J.: Weilet, 2003).

the nation or perhaps the presidency itself;[16] or even the
Jesuit order of the Roman Catholic Church, always good
for a conspiracy in Protestant eyes since the heady days
of the Counter-Reformation.[17] After all, were not the
conspirators Roman Catholics? Well, at least Dr. Samuel
A. Mudd and the Surratts were.

The common denominator in all these theories was
the not-too-subtle notion that John Wilkes Booth was
not wholly sane. This was the favorite assumption of the

16 Hanchett, *The Lincoln Murder Conspiracies*, 158-84, 210-
    33; Otto Eisenschiml, *Why Was Lincoln Murdered?* (New
    York: Grossett & Dunlap, 1937); *In the Shadow of Lincoln's
    Death* (New York: Wilfred Funk, 1940); Robert H Fowler,
    "Was Stanton Behind Lincoln's Murder [Ray Neff on L.C.
    Baker]," *Civil War Times Illustrated*, 3 (Aug. 1961), 4-13,
    16-23, and his "New Evidence in [the] Lincoln Murder
    Conspiracy," *ibid.*, 7 (Feb. 1965), 4-6, 8-11; Theodore
    Roscoe, *The Web of Conspiracy: The Complete Story of the
    Men Who Murdered Lincoln* (Englewood Cliffs: Prentice-
    Hall,1959); Vaughn Shelton, *Mask for Treason: The Lincoln
    Murder Trial* (Harrisburg: Stackpole Books, 1965); David
    Balsiger and Charles E. Sellier, *The Lincoln Conspiracy*
    (Los Angeles: Schick Sunn Classic Books, 1977).

17 Hanchett, *The Lincoln Murder Conspiracies*, 233-41;
    Charles Chiniquy, *Fifty Years in the Church of Rome*
    (rev. and complete ed., London: Robert Banks & Son,
    [1886]; Burke McCarthy, *The Suppressed Truth about the
    Assassination of Abraham Lincoln* (Philadelphia: Burke
    McCarthy, 1924); Emmett McLoughlin, *An Inquiry into
    the Assassination of Abraham Lincoln* (New York: Lyle
    Stuart, Inc., 1963; T. M. Harris, *Assassination of Lincoln* .
    . . (Boston: American Citizen Co., 1892).

time,[18] and has never been supplanted in the mind of the American people, who seem to like their assassins to be a brick short of a full load. Crazy killers do not threaten the inherent nobility of the American system of government. Booth's alleged insanity covered up a lot of sin--be it of omission or commission--personal, familial, or governmental.

The Booth family was instrumental in affirming Johnny's unbalanced mind. This absolved them of any complicity in their brother's evil act. Edwin Booth spoke for all when he asserted that, unlike the rest of them, Johnny "was a rattle-pated fellow, filled with Quixotic notions. . . , [a] wild-brained boy . . . insane [about secession]. . . ." Lincoln's 1864 reelection, Edwin maintained, "drove [poor ole Johnny] beyond the limits of reason."[19]

Lamentably, this ignored certain pronounced eccentricities of father Junius Brutus, mother Mary Ann, older brother June, older sisters Rosalie and Asia,

---

18 See, e.g., the statement of Joseph Bradley, Sr., in defense of accused conspirator John Surratt, Jr., quoted in Wilson, *John Wilkes Booth*, vii.

19 Edwin Booth to Nahum Capen, July 28th, 1881, in Stern, *Man Who Killed Lincoln*, 396-97. For Joseph A. Booth, see Junius Brutus Booth to Edwin Booth, October 20, 1863, in John Rhodehamel and Louise Taper (eds.), *"Right or Wrong, God Judge Me": The Writings of John Wilkes Booth* (Urbana: University of Illinois Press, 1997), 79n.5.

younger brother Joseph, and Edwin, himself, or as Booth crony and fellow actor Edwin Forrest once intemperately snorted, "All those goddam Booths were crazy."[20]

In sum, this leaves us as puzzled as Tad Lincoln, when he plaintively asked Union Secretary of the Navy Gideon Welles the morning after President Lincoln was shot: "Mr. Welles, *who* killed my father?"[21] In the answer to Tad Lincoln's question lies the key to clearing up the mystery of the rationale or ideology that motivated John Wilkes Booth to commit the first successful assassination of an American president.

No matter how family and chroniclers have superficially disparaged the motives of Booth the assassin, and thus implicitly agreed with Mencken's now-dated criticism of Southern culture (although black sociologist Thomas Sowell has recently brought Mencken's criticism up to date and applied it across racial lines, to the dismay of modern African American critics, in his tome, *Black Rednecks and White Liberals*),[22] there was one area, which historians somehow tend to forget, in which even Mencken admitted that the South had always led the nation and

---

20 Quoted in Stanley Kimmel, *The Mad Booths of Maryland*, 272.
21 Quoted in Bishop, T*he Day Lincoln Was Shot*, 297.
22 Thomas Sowell, *Black Rednecks and White Liberals* (San Francisco: Encounter Books, 2005), 1-64.

in which being a white, male, Southerner required an inordinate amount of smarts: political thought.

"It was [in the Slave South] that nearly all the political theories we still cherish and suffer under came to birth," Mencken noted dryly. Naturally, all of that occurred before the loss of the Southern War for Independence, often sweetly referred to in polite circles nowadays as "the Late Unpleasantnessî between the sections, and "The Calamity of Appomattox," that heart-breaking event that drove the South into "the clutch of the Yankee mortgage-clerk," as Mencken so aptly summed it up.[23]

What historians overlook in their haste to agree with Mencken's "Sahara of the Bozart," is the fact that John Wilkes Booth, far from being psychotic, physically ill, or manipulated by others, was a very typical antebellum white, male, Southerner in his political thought. This made him as predisposed to assassinating the Yankee president behind the lines as it made nearly one million other Southern, white males willing to destroy the North, and the Union, on the battlefield.[24]

---

23 H.L. Mencken, "The Calamity of Appomattox," *American Mercury*, Sept. 1930, pp. 29-31.

24 For the use of one million men as the number that served in the Confederate armies, see James M. McPherson, *Battle Cry of Freedom: The Civil War Era* (New York: Oxford University Press, 1988), 306n.41.

The key to understanding Booth's ideology is his so-called "Secession Crisis Speech of December 1860" (sometimes labeled the "Allow Me Speech," from its first words), actually an untitled essay never finished or delivered in a public forum.

Previously, this speech has been analyzed in three formats: in the excellent volume of Booth's published papers edited by archivist/curator John Rhodehamel and antiquarian collector Louise Taper;[25] and in two articles (one published, one not) by Professor of English Jeannine Clarke Dodels of Malcolm X University in Chicago.[26]

These three people correctly see this longest (at over 5,000 words) of Booth's often windy compositions (Dodels graciously called them "never succinct" and "weighed down with words")[27] as the most profound of his political testaments, but, led astray by the image of the nonintellectual South, they missed the point Booth was trying to make.

---

25 Rhodehamel and Taper (eds.), *Writings of John Wilkes Booth*, 47-69, including analysis.

26 Jeannine Clarke Dodels, "Water on Stone: A Study of John Wilkes Booth's 1860 Political Draft Preserved at the Players' Club NY," copy in hands of the author and her "John Wilkes Booth's Secession Crisis Speech of 1860" in Arthur Kincaid (ed.), *John Wilkes Booth, Actor: The Proceedings of a Conference Weekend in Bel Air, Maryland, May 1988* (North Leigh, Oxfordshire: Privately Published, 1988), 48-51.

27 Dodels, "Water on Stone," 20 (weighed), 22 (succinct).

Rhodehamel and Taper began by describing how Edwin Booth saved the speech, when it was accidentally discovered among Johnny's papers, after his death at Garrett's Farm in Virginia. They explained the tenor of his remarks by relying on the work of Professor Dodels, who skillfully placed Booth's speech in its historical, literary context and looked at it as a racist, pro-slavery reprise of Marc Anthony's "question and answer litany" from his funeral oration in William Shakespeare's *Julius Caesar*.

Once, Dodels almost stumbled over Booth's actual beliefs, when she, in passing, referred to the split between North and South as an argument involving "the reserved powers of the states in the Tenth Amendment" to the U.S. Constitution.[28] Alas, it was but a momentary lapse.

What, then, was the ideology that formed the basis of Booth's political thought? Well, it was state rights, as any decent high school history student will tell you. Not so. Actually, state rights and secession were the *alternative* to the Southern program to protect slavery before the Civil War. It was not until Abraham Lincoln and the Republican party threatened to destroy the real Southern program in

---

28 Dodels, "Water on Stone," 18 (question and answer); Dodels, "John Wilkes Booth's Secession Crisis Speech of 1860," in Kincaid (ed.), *John Wilkes Booth, Actor*, 49 (reserved powers); Rhodehamel and Taper (eds.), *Writings of John Wilkes Booth*, 52-53.

1861 that the South junked the Constitution of 1787[29] and opted for its second choice, the more radical concept of states rights and secession, copied directly from the Declaration of Independence.[30]

In truth, logic demanded that the reasoning employed for a positive program of protecting slavery within the Union could not be the same as the state rights that dissolved the Nation. They were actually antithetical— almost the exact reverse of each other, and John Wilkes Booth knew this.[31]

To begin with, one must realize, which even Booth may not have fully, that abolition of slavery in the

---

29 The pro-slavery nature of the original Constitution of 1787 is described in Alfred W. and Ruth G. Blumrosen, *Slave Nation: How Slavery United the Colonies and Sparked the American Revolution* (Naperville, Ills,: Sourcebooks, Inc., 2005) and Paul Finkelman, "Slavery and the Constitutional Convention: Making a Covenant with Death," in Richard Beeman, *et al.* (eds.), *Beyond Confederation: Origins of the Constitution and American National Identity* (Chapel Hill: University of North Carolina Press, 1987), 188-225, and Finkelman, "Garrison's Constitution: The Covenant of Death and How It Was Made," *Prologue: The Magazine of the National Archives*, 32 (2000), 230-45.

30 Kent Masterson Brown, "Secession: A Constitutional Remedy for the Breach of the Organic Law," *North & South*, 3 (August 2000), 12-21.

31 Arthur Bestor, "State Sovereignty and Slavery: A Reinterpretation of Pro-slavery Constitutional Doctrine, 1846-1860," Illinois State Historical Society, *Journal*, 53 (1960), 117-22.

existing states was *not* the issue. In fact, Lincoln and the Republicans were willing to guarantee slavery where it existed by a new irrevocable constitutional amendment (eventually agreed to by the free states of Ohio and Illinois, and the slave state of Maryland, before the war put an end to it in 1862).

Indeed, the only real way slavery could be destroyed in the states was by a constitutional amendment, which was practically impossible to achieve. This is because it takes three-fourths of the states to amend the Constitution, and the Slave South, being nearly half of the states, thus had a veritable veto. But, as Booth discerned, in agreeing to maintain slavery in the states where it existed, Lincoln and the Republicans never consented *not* to constrict or hamper the spread of slavery, elsewhere.[32]

If slavery in the states was not the issue, what was? As Booth correctly perceived, it was the *extraterritorial implications* of slavery as an institution, written into the Constitution of 1787.[33] This was revealed in the two

---

32 *Ibid.*, 122-27.
33 Contrary to the editor's argument in Don E. Fehrenbacher, *The Slaveholding Republic: An Account of the United States Government's Relations to Slavery* (New York: Oxford University Press, 2001), that the U.S. Constitution was neither a pro or anti-slavery document, anti-slavery Northerners came to fear that the Constitution was so tainted in favor of slavery that it might have to be replaced with a new document, until Republicans decided it was a

sectional issues that pestered the nation between the War with Mexico and the Civil War, the operations of the fugitive slave law, and slavery extension into the western territories of the United States.

What the South held, and Booth agreed with, basically, was that slaveholding states were justified in controlling the internal policies of non-slaveholding states whenever those policies adversely affected, even indirectly, the institution of slavery. This was the essence of extraterritoriality.[34]

---

good document that merely need to be purged of its pro-slavery sentiments. This was accomplished by William H. Whiting of the Adjutant General's Department in his 1862 treatise, *War Powers of the President*, later expanded into *War Powers under the Constitution of the United States*. See Michael Les Benedict, *Preserving the Constitution: Essays on Politics and the Constitution in the Reconstruction Era* (Fordham University Press, May 2006). See also, Harold M. Hyman, *A More Perfect Union: The Impact of the Civil War and Reconstruction on the Constitution* (Boston: Houghton Mifflin, 1975), 99-140; and Paul C. Nagel, *One Nation Indivisible: The Union in American Thought, 1776-1861* (New York: Oxford University Press, 1964). Also of interest are Richard Morris, *The Forging of the Union, 1781-1789* (Cambridge: Harper & Row, 1987), Donald L. Robinson, *Slavery in the Structure of American Politics, 1765-1821* (New York: Harcourt, Brace, Jovanovich, 1971); and Larry Gara, "Slavery and the Slave Power: A Crucial Distinction," *Civil War History*, 15 (1969), 5-18.

34 Bestor, "State Sovereignty and Slavery, 127-30.

Let's take the question of apprehending fugitive slaves, first.[35] John Wilkes Booth referred to the fugitive slave question in the last paragraph of his unfinished speech. This is unfortunate because the hand-written paragraph ended at the bottom of a page, leaving the modern reader to wonder, along with editors Rhodehamel and Taper, if that was all Booth wrote or if he continued the argument on pages since lost to history.[36]

Booth's allusion to the fugitive slave law revolved around the attempt of his Harford County, Maryland, neighbor, Edward Gorsuch (Booth erroneously called him Gorruge), to recover four runaway slaves. The bondsmen had stolen a quantity of Gorsuch's wheat, sold it to a local miller, and used their ill-gotten gains to finance their flight into Pennsylvania, a free state. As Booth put it, "[t]he father, two sons and the boy my playmate, came to [Pennsylvania] under the protection of the fugitive slave law (not only to recover their property, but to arrest the thieves who belonged to them). . . ."[37]

The slave-catchers, a legal posse led by a U.S. marshal and including the Gorsuches, found their quarry holed-up about 20 miles north of the Maryland border at

35 *Ibid.*, 130-40, for the fugitive problem in all of its manifestations.
36 Rhodehamel and Taper (eds.), *Writings of John Wilkes Booth*, 69n35.
37 *Ibid.*, 64, 69nn34-35.

Christiana. Ordered to surrender, the runaways and some black and white friends defended themselves and killed Edward Gorsuch and wounded one of his sons in a gun fight. The chastened posse retreated empty-handed.

The Federal government later brought 38 whites and blacks to trial on charges of treason, the largest treason trial in U.S. history. Defended by such anti-slavery luminaries as Thaddeus Stevens, Theodore A. Cuyler, and John Meredith, a Pennsylvania jury acquitted all defendants without even leaving the box to deliberate.[38]

Booth and all Southerners were angered at the results of this so-called Christiana Riot. It went against what they thought was a basic guarantee of the U.S. Constitution

---

38 *Ibid,.* 68-69nn33-34. On the Christiana Riot, see W. U. Hensel, *The Christiana Riot and Treason Trials of 1851* (Lancaster, Penn,: New Era Printing, 1851); Roderick Nash, "The Christiana Riot: An Evaluation of Its National Significance," *Journal of the Lancaster County Historical Society*, 65 (Spring, 1961), 65-91; Jonathan Katz, *Resistance at Christiana: The Fugitive Slave Rebellion, Christiana, Pennsylvania, September 11, 1851* (New York: Thomas Y. Crowell, 1974); Margaret Hope Bacon, *Rebellion at Christiana* (New York: Crown Publishers, Inc., 1975); Thomas P. Slaughter, *Bloody Dawn; the Christiana Riot and Racial Violence in the Antebellum North* (Oxford University Press, New York. 1991); Edward Steers, Jr., "Freedom Began Here," *North & South*, 1 (April 1998), 34-43; Stephanie Anderson, "Resistance at Christiana," *Central PA Magazine*, at http://www.centralpa.org/archives/02feb3christiana.html.

of 1787.[39] Found in Article IV, Section 2, Clause 3, the

---

39 Indeed, U.S. Senator Jefferson Davis of Mississippi correctly pointed out that there would have been no Union formed in 1787 without the fugitive clause (R.B. Way, "Was the Fugitive Slave Clause of the Constitution Necessary?" *Iowa Journal of History and Politics*, 5 [1907], 326-36).Written by Delegate Pierce Butler and pushed by Delegate Charles Cotesworth Pinckney (not to be confused with his younger, more liberal cousin, Charles Pinckney [Marty D. Matthews, *Forgotten Founder: The Life and Times of Charles Pinckney* (Columbia: University of South Carolina Press, 2004)]), the arch defenders of black slavery at the Constitutional Convention (1787), South Carolina and Georgia had made this one clause the essential thing for them to endorse changing away from the Articles of Confederation (1781). See Malcom Bell Jr., *Major Butler's Legacy: Five Generations of a Slaveholding Family* (Athens: University of Georgia Press, 1987), 66-97; Francis Coghlan, "Pierce Butler, 1744-1822: First Senator from South Carolina," *South Carolina Historical Magazine*, 78 (1977), 104-19; Marvin R. Zahniser, *Charles Cotesworth Pinckney: Founding Father* (Chapel Hill: University of North Carolina Press, 1967); M.E. Bradford, *Founding Fathers: Brief Lives of the Framers of the United States Constitution* (2nd ed., rev., Lawrence: University of Kansas Press, 1994), 194-201; Ernest M. Lander, "The South Carolinians at the Philadelphia Convention, 1787," *South Carolina Historical Magazine*, 57 (1956), 134-55; Sidney Ulmer, "The Role of Pierce Butler in the Constitutional Convention," *Review of Politics*, 22 (1960), 360-74; separate articles of Robert M. Weir, M.E. Bradford, and Robert E. Shalhope in "South Carolina and the U.S. Constitution: The First of Two Special Issues," *South Carolina Historical Magazine*, 73-113.

fugitive clause was critical to the Southern viewpoint on the extraterritoriality of slavery. It read:

> No Person held to Service or Labour in one State, under the laws thereof, escaping into another [State] shall, in Consequence of any Law or Regulation therein, be discharged from such Service or Labour, but shall be delivered up on Claim of the Party to whom such Service or Labour may be due.

This clause does not refer to criminal extradition, which is treated in Article IV, Section 2, Clause 2, in which the governor of a state has the right under state law to deny returning a person charged with "Treason, Felony or other Crime" to the state where an alleged crime was committed.[40]

The guaranteed fugitive return in Clause 3, called recaption, referred to slaves--those "held to Service or Labour" in the Constitution's more delicate language-- to whom bondage clung no matter where in the Union they might flee. The slave law of any slave state was to be enforced by the federal government in any other state in the Union, even if it were a free state.

---

40 *Annot. Constit.* (http://www.eco.freedom.org/ac92/ ac92pgix.shtml), 878-881. Standards of extradition are much more regularized nowadays. See Edwin Meese III, *et al.* (eds.), *The Heritage Guide to the Constitution* (Washington, D.C.: Regnery, 2005), 273-75.

But as Booth and the Slave South soon discovered, having a right in the Constitution and enforcing that right through the passage of a national law were two different things. The Fugitive Slave Law of 1793 arose from a quarrel over three white Virginians taking an accused slave, John Davis, out of Pennsylvania, which called the action the kidnapping of a free man of color.[41] Pennsylvania applied to Virginia to return the Negro and his kidnappers under Article IV, Section 2, Clause 2 of the U.S. Constitution. Virginia refused claiming that the correct constitutional provision was Clause 3, recaption, not felony kidnapping.

To solve this problem, Congress passed the Fugitive Slave Law of 1793. The statute authorized slave owners or their agents to apprehend fugitive slaves in any state or territory and required that owners apply to any state or federal judge for a certificate to take custody of accused runaways. Any citizen who sheltered an escaped slave could be fined $500 and sued for damages.[42]

---

41 Paul Finkelman, "The Kidnapping of John Davis and the Adoption of the Fugitive Slave Law of 1793," *Journal of Southern History*, 56 (1990), 397-422. The problem arose because Davis was taken from a part of western Pennsylvania that had been a part of Virginia until recently. Pennsylvania had freed its slaves in the area, while Virginia had not.

42 Such a lawsuit for damages is detailed in Paul Finkelman, "'The Law, and Not Conscience, Constitutes the Rule

The law was shot through with loopholes. It did not, for example, force state or federal judges to issue warrants of arrest, nor did it require federal marshals to assist owners. But a slaveholder or his or her agent could make an arrest and effect recaption on his own, if any level of government, local, state, or federal, refused to assist the process, which became an open invitation to kidnap any black, free or slave.

Although the Fugitive Slave Law of 1793 was one of the first major acts Congress passed under the new Constitution of 1787, the free states defied and violated it almost from the beginning by passing so-called personal liberty laws.

These acts made it possible for state authorities to circumvent the federal fugitive act by requiring *extra* state court warrants or jury trials before the federal arrest and recaption of suspected runaway slaves. Some, but not all, states made blacks citizens to protect their civil rights. In the 1840s the Liberty Party made personal liberty laws the center of its platform, declaring the federal fugitive slave act to be null and void under the higher laws of God, because, as abolitionist William Lloyd Garrison

---

of Action': The South Bend Fugitive Case and the Value of 'Justice Denied'." in Donald G. Nieman (ed.), *The Constitution, Law, and American Life: Critical Aspects of the Nineteenth Century Experience* (Athens: University of Georgia Press, 1992), 23-51.

once asserted, the pro-slavery U.S. Constitution was "a covenant with Death and an agreement with Hell." An Underground Railroad, that deliberately spirited slave runaways to the safety of British Canada, became commonplace in the free North.[43]

Like many Southerners, Booth was angered by Northern attempts to interfere with federal fugitive slave laws. "The [l]aws have not been enforced that would protect [S]outhern rights," Booth accused, while "others have been passed to [i]nfringe [upon those] rights." As to slaves, Booth asserted, "I know that the South has a right according to the [C]onstitution to keep and hold them." As to the South and runaways, Booth said, "we [in the North] have no right under [the C]onstitution to interfere with her or hers." Now "I would not have you [Northerners] violate our country's laws," Booth averred. "But I could wish you would prove to the [S]

---

43 These events are described in Thomas D. Morris, *Free Men All: The Personal Liberty Laws of the North, 1780-1861* (Baltimore: The Johns Hopkins University Press, 1974), 1-94. See also, Joseph L. Nogee, "The Prigg Case and Fugitive Slavery, 1842-1850," *Journal of Negro History*, 39 (1966), 198-209; Joseph C. Burke, "What Did the Prigg Decision Really Decide?" *Pennsylvania Magazine of History and Biography*, 93 (1969), 73-85; Sewell, Richard. *Ballots for Freedom: Antislavery Politics in the United States, 1837-1860*. New York: Oxford University Press, 1976.

outh with deeds, instead of words, that she shall have those rights. . . .which are her due."[44]

As Booth and all Americans were aware, interference by the Northern states with runaway recaption had inevitably led to a U.S. Supreme Court case. In 1837, the year before Booth was born, Edward Prigg and a posse of slave-catchers, representing Margaret Ashmore, a Maryland slaveholder from Booth's home county of Harford, applied to a Pennsylvania justice of the peace for a warrant to seize certain runaways belonging to Ashmore's plantation estate, who had escaped five years earlier.

The slaves were a mother and her children. Prigg brought them before a state judge in York, Pennsylvania, and asked for the right to extradite them to Maryland. The judge was appalled that a mother and her children might be re-enslaved and refused permission, especially since Ashmore's recently deceased father had let them live apart from the Maryland plantation in Pennsylvania in a form of quasi-freedom for some years. Nonetheless, Prigg smuggled them back into Maryland without the required Pennsylvania state legal papers.

A Pennsylvania grand jury immediately returned an indictment against Prigg and his possemen for kidnapping.

---

44 Rhodehamel and Taper (eds.), *Writings of John Wilkes Booth*, 57.

The Pennsylvania governor applied to Maryland for criminal extradition under Article IV, Section 2, Clause 2 of the U.S. Constitution. The governor of Maryland refused to honor Pennsylvania's request and sent the whole matter to the Maryland state legislature. The legislature passed a series of resolutions supporting the absolute right of recaption under Article IV, Section 2, Clause 3.

In 1838, under prior agreement with Pennsylvania, only Prigg surrendered to Pennsylvania authorities, who tried and convicted him. Prigg was allowed to be free on bond, while prearranged appeals sent the case to the U.S. Supreme Court, as Prigg v. Pennsylvania.

Led by Associate Justice Joseph Story of Massachusetts (never a pro-slave advocate, by any means),[45] the U.S.

---

45 E.g., Story ruled to free the slaves in the Amistad Case. See Howard Jones, *Mutiny on the* Amistad: *The Saga of a Slave Revolt and Its Impact on American Abolition, Law, and Diplomacy.* (New York: Oxford University Press, 1987; revised ed. 1997). See also, James McClellan, *Joseph Story and the American Constitution: A Study in Political and Legal Thought with Selected Writings* (Norman: University of Oklahoma, 1971); Robert M. Cover, *Justice Accused: Antislavery and the Judicial Process* (New Haven; Yale University Press, 1975); Kent Newmyer, *Supreme Court Justice Joseph Story: Statesman of the Old Republic* (Chapel Hill: University of North Carolina Press, 1985); Alan Watson, *Joseph Story and the Comity of Errors: A Case Study in the Conflict of Laws* (Athens: University of Georgia Press, 1992); Barbara Holden-Smith, "Lords of

Supreme Court ruled (6-1, two members missing) in 1842 that the fugitive slave clause was solely a federal responsibility that could not be interfered with by the states. The U.S. Constitution, which was superior to state law, whenever they conflicted, guaranteed that a slaveholder or his or her agents had an "absolute right" to take "immediate possession" of runaway slave property, Story said, without necessarily involving local authorities, no matter where in the United States it was found. Hence Prigg violated no valid state law.

This was because slavery had an extraterritorial effect superior to local laws. The only limits to this extraterritorial right, according to Story, was that any removal of slave property be accomplished without a breech of the peace (an old English common law proscription noted by Blackstone), or what the U.S. Supreme Court vaguely defined as "illegal violence." Prigg had met that standard. He was freed and his bond returned.[46]

---

the Lash, Loom, and Law: Justice Story, Slavery, and Prigg v. Pennsylvania," *Cornell Law Review,* 78 (1993), 1086ff.; Paul Finkelman, "Sorting Out Prigg v. Pennsylvania," *Rutgers Law Journal,* 24 (1993), 605-55; *id.,* Prigg v. Pennsylvania: Understanding Justice Story's Pro-slavery Nationalism," *1996 Journal of Supreme Court History,* 2 (1997), 51-46; and *id.,* "Story Telling on the Supreme Court: Prigg v. Pennsylvania and Justice Story's Judicial Nationalism," *1994 Supreme Court Review (1995),* 247-94.

46 See Prigg v. Pennsylvania, (1842), 16 Peters at 539.

Justice Story and the Court had ruled solely on the legal aspects of the fugitive slave issue, devoid of any moral or ethical questions. But every personal liberty law in the North had been struck down and all that remained was the original Fugitive Slave Act of 1793. In Booth's words, the Slave South had, at last, seemingly received "*her due.*"[47]

But the Southern states saw this old legislation as proven inadequate. In 1850, after the Annexation of Texas and the War with Mexico, the Slave South demanded that a new Draconian fugitive slave act, written by Senator James M. Mason of Virginia, be passed as a part of the Compromise of 1850.[48] It would toughen the old law of

47 Morris, *Free Men All*, 94-106.
48 On the complicated issues facing the nation in 1850, see Holman Hamilton, *Prologue to Conflict: The Crisis and Compromise of 1850* (Lexington: University of Kentucky Press, 1964); Frank H. Hodder, "The Authorship of the Compromise of 1850," *Mississippi Valley Historical Review*, 22 (1936), 525-36; George D. Harmon, "Douglas and the Compromise of 1850," Illinois State Historical Society, *Journal*, 21 (1929), 477-79; Jean H. Baker, *Affairs of Party: The Political Culture of Northern Democrats in the Mid-Nineteenth Century* (Ithaca: Cornell University Press, 1983); Joel Sibley, *The Shrine of Party: Congressional Voting Behavior, 1841-1852* (Pittsburgh: University of Pittsburgh Press, 1967); Elbert B. Smith, *The Presidencies of Zachary Taylor and Millard Fillmore*. (Lawrence: University Press of Kansas, 1988); Merrill D. Petersen, *The Great Triumvirate: Webster, Clay, and Calhoun* (New York: Oxford University Press, 1987).

1793, immeasurably. This was the law that Booth knew and referred to in his 1860 speech.

To replace heretofore uncooperative state courts, Mason's act established special federal fugitive slave courts with federal commissioners who acted as justices of the peace. To avoid interference from hesitant Yankee citizens, no jury trial was to be had. The only evidence to be seen by a commissioner was the affidavit from the wronged slaveholder. No black testimony was allowed. If the commissioner ruled the Negro in question to be a slave, he received twice the court fees ($10) than if he ruled the black to be free, which gave the appearance of a bribe to rule for slavery.

Finally, the commissioner's ruling was to be a complete answer to any writ of *habeas corpus* in any court, state or federal. If anyone interfered with the recaption process, he or she was liable to a $1,000 fine and six months in jail. If any slave escaped during such interference, the convicted vigilante had to pay, in addition to other punishment, another $1,000 per escaped slave.

Any federal law enforcement officer who failed zealously to secure the slave in question and allowed him or her to escape or be freed by extra-legal action was liable for the slave's market value back home in the South. (By the way, any citizen was subject to be drafted off the streets as a part of a federal slave-catching *posse comitatus*, and come under this sanction). It was this law that Booth's neighbor Gorsuch employed to pursue his runaways to Christiana.

The essence of the Fugitive Slave Law of 1850 was that it did not allow the right in property to a Negro to be determined anywhere but in the state of the accused slave's origin. As one Southern representative from Alabama put it: "We want the *substance*, not the mere *shadow* of our rights." Mason's new Fugitive Slave Act of 1850 was basically a law of guaranteed recaption, as demanded by the U.S. Constitution, Article IV, Section 2, Clause 3.[49]

As Southerners said, and Booth asserted in one of his most often quoted sentiments, "[t]his country was formed for the *white* not for the black man."[50] Indeed, the Constitution made no mention of African-Americans, except as fugitives to be returned, as three-fifths of a person to be counted for purposes of direct taxation and representation of white slaveholders in Congress, and as goods to be traded internationally until January 1, 1808.[51] Blacks were not (and did not have the rights

49 Morris, *Free Men All*, 130-47.
50 Rhodehamel and Taper (eds.), *The Writings of John Wilkes Booth*, 125.
51 The effect of these and other compromises on slavery gave the South a preeminent position in early America. See Garry Wills, *"Negro President": Jefferson and the Slave Power* (Boston: Houghton Miflin Co., 2003), 1-13.

of) American citizens, as the Fugitive Slave Act of 1850 clearly demonstrated.

In response to the passage of the Fugitive Slave Law, the Northern states soon passed new personal liberty acts that agreed with the part of the Prigg decision that said that the states need not help the federal government in returning accused slaves, so long as they did not interfere with the process. The new personal liberty laws forbade any state official to assist in *any* manner federal law enforcement agents, slave-catchers, or slave-owners in the recovery of runaway slaves.[52]

Nonetheless, inspired by the moral question of the assumption of freedom for all persons regardless of race, individual Northerners began to interfere with the operations of slave-catchers and federal marshals, as the Christiana Incident involving Booth's neighbor, Edward Gorsuch, showed.[53]

---

52 Paul Finkelman, "Prigg v. Pennsylvania and Northern State Courts: Anti-slavery Use of a Pro-slavery Decision," *Civil War History*, 25 (1979), 5-35.

53 Larry Gara, "Results of the Fugitive Slave Law," *Civil War Times Illustrated*, 2 (October 1963), 30-37; Norman L. Rosenberg, "Personal Liberty Laws and Sectional Crisis," *Civil War History*, 17 (1971), 25-45. From the other side, see Stanley W. Campbell, *The Slave Catchers: Enforcement of the Fugitive Slave Acts* (Chapel Hill: University of North Carolina Press, 1970), and Russell B. Nye, *Fettered Freedom: Civil Liberties and the Slavery Controversy, 1930-1860*. East Lansing: Michigan State College Press, 1949.

But nothing beat newspaper editor Sherman Booth's (no relation to the Maryland Booths) rescue of a runaway slave, Joshua Glover, in Wisconsin in 1854. Glover had been captured by slave catchers, after a violent encounter that left him bruised and bleeding. Sherman Booth led a group of "concerned citizens," who released Glover from captivity and spirited him away into Canada. U.S. Marshal Stephen V.R. Ableman then arrested Sherman Booth, who had bragged of his role in his newspaper.

Hauled before the federal commissioner, Sherman Booth was indicted and prosecuted for violating the Fugitive Slave Law of 1850. Twice, Sherman Booth managed to get a writ of *habeas corpus* from friendly state judges, in spite of the ban on such devices in the federal law. In the process, the Wisconsin state courts declared the federal fugitive slave act to be unconstitutional and interposed the state's authority between Sherman Booth and the federal government.[54]

By 1859, the case had reached the U.S. Supreme Court, Chief Justice Roger B. Taney of Maryland presiding, as Ableman v. Booth.[55] A strict interpreter of

54 Joseph Schafer, "Stormy Days in Court—The Booth Case," *Wisconsin Magazine of History*, 20 (1936), 89-110.
55 On Taney, see Charles W. Smith, Jr., *Roger B. Taney: Jacksonian Jurist* (Chapel Hill: University of North Carolina Press, 1936); Carl Brent Swisher, *Roger B. Taney* (New York: Macmillan, 1935); H.H. Walker Lewis, *Without Fear or Favor: A Biography of Chief Justice Roger B.*

the Constitution rather a proslave advocate, as modern historians often wrongly assert,[56] Taney was a slaveholder who found slavery distasteful in the long run and emancipated his slaves before the Civil War, providing for their upkeep. Speaking for a unanimous court (9-0), Taney overruled every point that Sherman Booth's defenders in Wisconsin made.

Taney admitted that Wisconsin was sovereign (supreme political power independent of and not limited by any other entity) within its state boundaries. Yet, Taney said, that state sovereignty was conditionally limited and voluntarily restricted through the state's own Constitution and by adhering to the supremacy clause of the U.S. Constitution, as soon as a state joined the Union.[57] What Taney and the court did was to declare once again that Article IV, Section 2, Clause 3, gave an

---

Taney (Boston: Houghton Mifflin, 1965); Paul Finkelman, "Hooted Down the Page of History?: Reconsidering the Greatness of Chief Justice Taney," *1994 Journal of the Supreme Court History* (1995), 83-102.

56 McPherson, *Battle Cry of Freedom*, 173, referencing Don E. Fehrenbacher, "Roger B. Taney and the Sectional Crisis, *Journal of Southern History*, 43 (1977), 555-66. See also, Finkelman, "'Hooted Down the Pages of History'," 97.

57 For a good explanation of this principle by a foreign sympathizer of the Confederacy, see Charles Priestley (ed.), "A Philosopher's Defense of the Confederacy: Jermyn Cowell to Henry Sidgwick, September 1863," *North & South*, 9 (May 2006), 82-88, especially 85.

extraterritorial power to the Southern slave states that would be enforced solely by the federal courts. Taney did not declare the supremacy of national policy, but exactly the reverse. He denied any discretionary, policy-making functions to the federal government in the matter of slavery alone.

The U.S. Constitution gave extraterritorial powers to slave states only, Taney said, states that possessed that peculiar type of property. That non-slaveholding states had no extraterritorial powers was a result of their voluntarily freeing their slaves, a perfectly legal act for any *state* to do.[58]

So, John Wilkes Booth was correct to see the fugitive slave issue as a key to the Slave South's political position before the Civil War. He was accurate to see the resistance to neighbor Gorsuch as unlawful, and the Northern states' support of resistance as contrary to the spirit of the U.S. Constitution, the Compromise of 1850, and the Fugitive Slave Acts.

But the concept of extraterritoriality was to play an even bigger role in another pre-Civil War issue—the expansion of slavery into the western territories, particularly after the American victory in the War with Mexico. It was here that the Southern view of extraterritoriality revealed itself

58 Morris, *Free Men All*, 166-85; Bestor, "State Sovereignty and Slavery," 140-47. See also, Ableman v. Booth (1859), 21 Howard at 506.

as a blatant tenet of domestic political power to promote the creation of new slave states in something called the non-exclusion doctrine.[59]

In his draft speech of 1860, John Wilkes Booth understood what the right to carry slaves into the West meant. "What right have you to exclude [S]outhern rights from the ter[r]itor[ies]?" he demanded. "Because you are the strongest? I have as much right to carry my slave into the ter[r]itor[ies] as you have to carry your paid servant or your children," Booth asserted.[60]

As Booth and the Slave South were aware, the ability of slaveholding Americans to move west with their slaves into the territories and to hold them and exploit their labor there was an extraterritorial right. They would be living beyond their state of origin, expecting protection of their slave property, as if they were still at home in the South. The problem arose because territorial government was not really mentioned in the Constitution. Only state and federal government were. But the Union had almost always had three elements, state, federal, and territorial.

Booth, and indeed most Americans, North or South, were cognizant of the fact that the real question was which entity (state, federal or territorial) was to exercise control

---

59 Bestor, "State Sovereignty and Slavery," 147-62, for a discussion of slavery in the territories.
60 Rhodehamel and Taper (eds.), *Writings of John Wilkes Booth*, 64.

over domestic social policy, the so-called police power, involving the health, safety, welfare, and morals of the general population, which included local slave codes.[61] The U.S. Constitution left this up to the states under the Tenth Amendment, but no real Constitutionally defined government existed in the territories, which were not co-equal to the states.[62]

---

61 Police power was a term first coined by Chief Justice Taney in another context back in 1827 (as an attorney practicing before the Sup. Ct.), see Charles Warren, *The Supreme Court in United States History, 1789-1918* (2 vols., Boston: Little, Brown & Co., 1922), I, 695 n.2. A good listing of he state police powers is in Forrest McDonald, *States' Rights and the Union: Imperium in Imperio, 1776-1876* (Lawrence: University of Kansas Press, 2000), 223.

62 This is where the South differed from Lincoln and Northern Democrat and Lincoln rival in Illinois, U.S. Senator Stephen A. Douglas. Lincoln backed Squatter Sovereignty, the notion of former Democratic presidential candidate Lewis Cass that the slavery question in a territory could be decided by the territorial legislature. Lincoln forced Douglas to abandon his Popular Sovereignty, the Southern Non-exclusion Doctrine, in the Lincoln-Douglas Debates of 1858, with the so-called Freeport Doctrine. In this, Douglas stated that a territorial legislature could deny slavery legal protection and thus its efficacy at any time before it became a state. This won Douglas the U.S. Senate seat from Illinois in 1858 but cost Douglas support for the presidency in 1860 and guaranteed Lincoln's nomination by the Republicans as a moderate anti-slavery man. See Roy Basler (ed.), *The Collected Works of Abraham Lincoln* (9 vols., New Brunswick: Rutgers University Press, 1953), III, 43 (Freeport Question), 51-52 (Freeport Doctrine).

The question of free or pro-slave states had not been much of a problem prior to the War with Mexico, as free and slave states had been admitted into the Union in pairs, which kept a North-South equilibrium in the U.S. Senate. True, there had been a flare-up in 1820, when the admission of Missouri threatened to tilt the balance toward the Southern slave states, but this had been dampened when Massachusetts allowed its northern-most county to be admitted as the free and separate state of Maine.

Hereafter, according to this so-called Missouri Compromise, any new territories in the Louisiana Purchase (1803) would be free states if they were incorporated north of the line 36°30', the southern boundary of Missouri. This meant that slavery expansion in the West would be restricted to the territories of Arkansas and the Indian Nations (essentially modern Oklahoma) between 1820 and 1845.[63]

---

63 For the Missouri Compromise, see Glover Moore, *The Missouri Controversy, 1819-1821* (Lexington: University of Kentucky Press, 1966); Richard Holbrook Brown, *The Missouri Compromise: Political Statesmanship or Unwise Evasion?* (Boston: Heath, 1964); Tristram Potter Coffin, *The Missouri Compromise* (Boston: Little Brown, 1947); Frank H. Hodder, ìSide Lights on the Missouri Compromises,î in American Historical Association, Reports (1909), pp. 151-161. On an congressionally-agreed-upon exception to the 36°30' rule concerning the Platte Region, see H. Jason Combs, "The South's Slave Culture Transplanted to

But the Annexation of Texas (1845) and War with Mexico (1846-48) opened up a whole lot of territory below the Missouri Compromise line and south of the Louisiana Purchase, as Booth or any educated person who could read a map easily perceived. The North, in effect, had fought a war to open up a vast area in the Mexican Cession of the American Southwest to be potential slave states, under the terms of the Missouri Compromise.

Northern congressmen had cried foul even before the war started. They introduced the Wilmot Proviso in 1846, as the war began, proposing that any territorial concession from Mexico would be without slavery. The South demurred and, although the Wilmot Proviso passed the Yankee-dominated U.S. House of Representatives, Southern senators blocked it in the equally divided U.S. Senate,[64] holding out for the non-exclusion of slavery in all territories as an extraterritorial right.

---

the Western Frontier," *The Professional Geographer: Forum and Journal of the Association of American Geographers*, 56 (2004), 361-71.

64 Both Florida and Texas had been admitted in before Iowa and Wisconsin came in during the War with Mexico, giving the South a temporary majority in the Senate. See Paul Finkelman, "Dred Scott, Slavery, and the Politics of Law," *Hamline Law Review*, 20 (1996), 1-42, at 34n119. Until 1858, however, the South was usually assisted in its control of both houses of Congress by northerners sympathetic to slavery, either morally or politically. See Leonard L. Richards, *The Slave Power: The Free North*

Actually, there had been no federal territories in the West until the original thirteen states ceded their western lands to the federal government as part of the ratifying process of our first national Constitution, the Articles of Confederation of 1781. This land cession between the Appalachian Mountains and the Mississippi River was not complete when the Constitution of 1787 was drafted, so the Constitution itself limited federally controlled territories to the District of Columbia and various military installations (dockyards, arsenals, magazines, and forts) that the federal government *purchased from the states* with their consent.[65]

But it was obvious that Congress somehow would have to administer the newly-ceded state lands in the West, and the Constitution allowed for such governance,[66] without defining what territories were or what "needful rules and regulations" like a slave code might be demanded there. The Slave South argued that the exercise of this police power was the prerogative of a sovereign. The citizens of a territory lacked complete sovereignty because they shared

---

and Southern Domination, 1780-1860 (Baton Rouge: Louisiana State University Press, 2000).

65 Article I, Section 8, Clause 17.

66 Article IV, Section 3, Clause 2.

it with the federal government under the provisions of the Land Ordinance of 1787.[67]

Congress, without an outright delegation by the states of their sovereign power over the territories, had no sovereignty there, either. Indeed, as Professor Dodles had obliquely hinted, the Tenth Amendment stated that, in a government of delegated powers as existed under the Constitution, the local police powers were reserved only to sovereign states admitted into the Union.

But it was obvious that each individual state could not enforce its own concept of police powers in any or all territories. That would create rank confusion. The solution was for the states to allow the federal government

---

67 Ray Allen Billington, "The Historians of the Northwest Ordinance," Illinois State Historical Society, *Journal*, 40 (1947), 347-413; Jack E. Eblen, "The Origins of the United States Colonial System: The Ordinance of 1787," *Wisconsin Magazine of History*, 51 (1968), 294-314; Frederick D. Stone, "The Ordinance of 1787," *Pennsylvania Magazine of History and Biography*, 25 (1938), 167-80; Staughton Lynd, "The Compromise of 1787," *Political Science Quarterly*, 81 (1966), 225-50; Merrill Jensen, "The Creation of the National Domain, 1781-1784," *Mississippi Valley Historical Review*, 26 (1939), 323-42; T.C. Pease, "The Ordinance of 1787," *ibid.*, 25 (1938): 167-80; Frederick D. Williams (ed.), Northwest Ordinance: Essays on Its Formulation, Provisions, and Legacy (Lansing: Michigan State University Press, 1989). See also, Paul Finkelman, "Slavery and the Northwest Ordinance: A Study in Ambiguity," *Journal of the Early Republic*, 6 (1986), 343-70.

to function as their agent. The federal government would act on the slavery question in the territories not as the government of the *United* States but as the trustee of the *States* united.

That is to say, the federal government, in the matter of slavery in the territories alone, would act as a mere deputy, a representative to give every state's laws an extraterritorial effect. There was no discretion or deliberation allowed here. The federal government was to administrate, not legislate.

The Constitution, of course, specifically said which laws had an extraterritorial character. The only state laws that had extraterritorial effect were the laws pertaining to slavery through the fugitive recaption clause of the Constitution, Article IV, Section 2, Clause 3.

This so-called non-exclusion doctrine (*i.e.*, no prior exclusion of slavery in any western territories before statehood) paid off big in 1857 in the case of Scott v. Sanford,[68] which influenced John Wilkes Booth and every

---

68 Dred Scott v. John F.A. Sanford, *et al.*, 19 Howard at 393. See Bestor, "State Sovereignty and Slavery," 167-72; Paul Finkelman, "What Did the Dred Scott Case Really Decide?" *Reviews in American History*, 7 (1979), 368-74. See also, Robert M.Cover, *Justice Accused: Antislavery and Judicial Process* (New Haven: Yale University Press, 1975); Don E. Fehrenbacher, *The Dred Scott Case: Its Significance in American Law and Politics* (New York: Oxford University Press, 1978); Paul Finkelman, *An Imperfect Union: Slavery,*

other American of that era. Dred Scott was a slave in Missouri owned by an army surgeon, Dr. John Emerson, who had legally bought him while serving at Jefferson Barracks below St. Louis.

As an army doctor, Emerson changed duty stations frequently. Among others, he went to Ft. Armstrong, at Rock Island, Illinois, a free territory under the Northwest Ordinance of 1787 and a free state since its admission to the Union in 1818; then to Ft. Snelling (present-day Minneapolis), Minnesota, a free territory under the 1820 Missouri Compromise.

At each post, Emerson took his slave, Dred Scott, with him. In Minnesota, Dred Scott fell in love and married another slave, Harriett Robinson (whom Dr. Emerson kindly bought), with whom Scott had a daughter, Eliza, who was born on a Mississippi River steamboat between the free territory of Iowa (under the

---

Federalism, and Comity (Chapel Hill: University of North Carolina Press, 1981); Vincent C. Hopkins, *Dred Scott's Case* (New York: Fordham University Press, 1951); Harold M. Hyman, and William Wiecek. *Equal Justice under Law: Constitutional Development, 1835-1875* (New York: Harper & Row, 1982); Stanley I. Kutler (ed.), *The Dred Scott Decision: Law or Politics?* (Boston: Houghton Mifflin Co., 1967); E. I. McCormick, "Justice Campbell and the Dred Scott Decision," *Mississippi Valley Historical Review*, 19 (1933), 565-71; Frank H. Hodder, "Some Phases of the Dred Scott Case," *Mississippi Valley Historical Review*, 16 (June 1929), 3-22.

Missouri Compromise) and the free state of Illinois. Then Dr. Emerson returned to St. Louis, where he obligingly died (for the sake of our story) in 1843 at age 40 from the advanced stages of syphilis, passing his property, including Dred Scott and his family, to Mrs. Irene Emerson and their newborn daughter (both of whom, evidently, remained free of the disease).

Mrs. Emerson permitted her brother, John F.A. Sanford,[69] to administer the estate. Sanford regularly hired Dred Scott out to other people, a common practice, particularly in the Border South. Scott even went to Mexico during the war, a country that had banned slavery in 1821, as a slave hired out to a U.S. Army officer.

When he returned to St. Louis after the war, Scott asked to buy himself and his family out of slavery. Mrs. Emerson, through Sanford, refused. Scott sued for his freedom, claiming that he had falsely been enslaved in a free territory and in a free state and in a free country.

Scott lost his suit in the local court, but won it in the Missouri district court. Sanford, claiming Scott was a citizen of Missouri and he a citizen of New York (where

---

69 Sanford was the principal representative in St. Louis for John Jacob Astor's American Fur Company out of New York City. See Hiram M. Chittenden, *The American Fur Trade of the Far West* (2 vols., Lincoln: University of Nebraska Press, 1986 reprint of 1935 edition), I, 373n5. But he administered the Emerson estate from New York.

he had been born), took the case to federal court. By now the law suit had become a *cause célèbre* and big name Republican lawyers, like Edward Bates (Lincoln's future attorney general) and Frank Blair, Jr. (his brother, Montgomery, would be Lincoln's postmaster general), volunteered to represent Scott. Scott lost again in the U.S. circuit court, and appealed the case to the U.S. Supreme Court.

Meanwhile, to thoroughly complicate things, Mrs. Emerson got remarried to a Yankee abolitionist congressman, moved to Massachusetts, and, imbued with love in more aspects than one, saw the error of her prior slaveholding ways, and freed Dred Scott and his family. In reality there was no real case, because Scott would now go free no matter what the U.S. Supreme Court ruled.

But the legal myth of Scott's continued slavery was maintained until the law suit ran its course, with the St. Louis County sheriff administering the hiring and putting the wages Scott earned in a trust to be paid to which ever side won the litigation. The case of Scott v. Sanford was decided in March 1857. At that time, the U.S. Supreme Court had nine members (the same nine who would rule unanimously in Ableman v. Booth two years later). They were seven Jacksonian Democrats (five of whom were slaveholders), one Whig, and one Republican.

Hence, it was no surprise that the court ruled seven to two that Dred Scott was still a slave. But no one could agree as to why. Each judge wrote a separate opinion, so it was the ruling of the Chief Justice, Roger B. Taney of Maryland, concurred with in part by five other associate judges, that became the accepted majority opinion.

Taney said that blacks were not citizens of the state of Missouri and never had been. Hence Scott could not even bring suit in state or federal court. Indeed, Taney noted that even most free states refused to allow Negro citizenship (which at that time was a state matter before the Fourteenth Amendment made citizenship a federal question in 1867). Taney should have stopped there and thrown the case out of court. But he and the Slave South had been waiting a long time for this opportunity, and Taney was not going to let it go to waste.

A slave's mere residence in or transit through a free state or a free territory did not free a slave, Taney went on. This was because Article IV, Section 2, Clause 3 of the U.S. Constitution gave slavery an extraterritorial quality that had to be enforced everywhere in the nation.

Only when a territory gained its complete, undivided sovereignty through becoming a state, could it legislate against slavery within it own boundaries, Taney ruled. Until then, Congress and the federal government were but trustees or temporary caretakers to administer all extraterritorial powers of slavery. This meant that the Missouri Compromise of no slavery in *some* territories was Unconstitutional. So was the Wilmot Proviso of no slavery extension into *any* territories.

This, then, was the extraterritoriality of slavery promised by the U.S. Constitution--guaranteed fugitive recaption and no prior limits to slavery extension into the territories. Booth's own 1860 rough-draft speech was right in line with the South's two concepts of the extraterritoriality of slavery, and policies endorsed by a majority of the U.S. Supreme Court in three important decisions.[70]

---

70 In 1858, Lincoln used a biblical theme to show that he understood and opposed the extraterritoriality of slavery, "a house divided against itself cannot stand. . . . Either the *opponents* of slavery will arrest the further spread of it, and place it where the public mind shall rest in the belief that it is in course of ultimate extinction," Lincoln maintained, "or its *advocates* will push it forward, till it shall become lawful in *all* states, *old* as well as *new—North* as well as *South*." Lincoln would have none of it. "I believe that this nation cannot endure, permanently half *slave* and half *free*," he posited. "I do not expect the Union to be *dissolved*—I do not expect the house to *fall*—but I *do* expect it will cease to be divided." Basler (ed.), *The Collected Works of Abraham Lincoln*, II, 461-62 (quotes), 464-67. See also, Alexander Gigante, "Slavery and a House Divided," at http://afroamhistory.about.com/library/prm/blhousedivided. htm; Paul Finkelman, "The Nationalization of Slavery: A Counter-factual Approach to the 1860s," *Louisiana Studies*, 14 (Fall 1975), 213-40.

Hence, it is no surprise that uncomprehending modern commentators brush off way too quickly one of the most important statements Booth made. "I am a [N]orthern man," he said. "But unlike most Northerners, I have looked upon both sides of this question."[71]

What Booth was saying here was that he was an *American*, who wanted to stand by the Constitution as interpreted by the U.S. Supreme Court in Prigg and Ableman (on fugitive slave return) and Dred Scott (on the extension of slavery into the West). He was for the extraterritoriality of slavery *within* the Union.

"The [S]outh wants justice," Booth proclaimed, "[she] has waited for it long, [and] she will wait no longer."[72] But, Booth backtracked quickly, sensing he may have crossed an invisible line here, "I don't mean to admit that the [S]outh should [secede]. [N]or do I believe a state can [secede] without revolution & blood-shed. But," Booth said, "the foundation of this great [U]nion was justice & [e]qual rights [for whites]."[73]

Booth then pledged, "I will not fight for [secession]. No[,] I will not fight for disunion. But I will fight with all

---

71   Rhodehamel and Taper (eds.), *Writings of John Wilkes Booth*, 55. Rhodehamel and Taper are typical in their analysis of this, 64n.3, seeing Booth as unashamedly pandering to a Philadelphia audience, and covering up his real Southern leanings.

72   *Ibid.*, 57.

73   *Ibid.*, 61-62.

my heart and soul, even if there [is] not a man to back me, for [e]qual rights and justice to the [white] South."[74]

On what did Booth blame the sectional crisis over secession in 1860? "I tell you[,]" Booth cried, agreeing with President James Buchanan's recent annual message to Congress,[75] "the Abolition doctrine is the fire which[,] if allowed to rage[,] will consume the house and crush us all beneath its ruins. . . . It is a fire lighted and fan[n]ed by Northern fanaticism."[76]

Booth then questioned the patriotism of abolition's supporters. "Do you not call it treason for men to entertain & advocate opinions which are hurtful to their country, which will destroy her peace and her prosperity[?] . . . Then[,] what are they who preach the Abolitionist doctrine [and] who have in doing so[,] nigh destroyed our country[?]" Booth supplied his own answer, "I call them traitors."[77]

---

74 *Ibid.*, 55.

75 John B. Moore (ed.), *The Works of James Buchanan* (12 vols, Philadelphia: J.P. Lippincott, 1910), IX, 754.

76 Rhodehamel and Taper (eds.), *Writings of John Wilkes Booth*, 59.

77 *Ibid.*, 56. Booth's hostility to the abolitionists may have been spurred by his witnessing the execution of John Brown. See Glenn Tucker, "John Wilkes Booth at the John Brown Hanging," *Lincoln Herald*, 78 (Spring 1976), 3-11, for Booth's presence at the execution; and David S. Reynolds, "John Brown, the Election of 1860, and the

He further condemned the abolitionists [in this he incorrectly included those anti-slavery expansionists like Lincoln, who wanted to save the West for exploitation by white settlers only][78] for failing to comprehend the *racial* magnitude of the *social* side of slavery. "[I]nstead of looking upon slavery as a sin (m[e]rely because I have none)[,]" Booth explained, "I hold it to be a happiness for [the slaves,] and a social & political blessing for us [whites]."[79]

"What is to be done?" Booth asked, rhetorically. Well, Booth said, "there are m[a]ny who are for instant coercion [of the South back into the Union]. That is madness. The first attempt at force will be the cue for every [S]outhern state to aid [the already-seceded state of South Carolina],"[80] Booth theorized, making him more prescient than the new Lincoln administration would be

---

Civil War," *North & South*, 9 (March 2006), 78-88, for the possible political theory.

78 Eugene H. Berwanger *The Frontier against Slavery: Western Anti-Negro Prejudice and the Slavery Extension Controversy* (Urbana: University of Illinois Press, 1967).

79 *Ibid.*, 62.

80 *Ibid.* See also, Steven A. Channing, *Crisis of Fear: Secession in South Carolina* (New York: Norton, 1970); Dwight L. Dumond, *The Secession Movement, 1860-1861* (New York: Octagon Books, 1963, orig. 1931).

a few months later (unless one suspects Lincoln really wanted the war he got).[81]

"We must not use force against [the South]," Booth declared. "If we do then we are greater tyrants [t]han George the 3d ever was towards our [Founding F]athers! Yet [the South] must be brought back [into the Union] and it must be done with compromise."[82]

Amazingly, after all his argument in favor of the South's extraterritorial rights to slavery extension, Booth contradicted himself. His solution to the secession crisis was that of U.S. Senator John J. Crittenden of Kentucky--to extend the Missouri Compromise line from Indian Territory to the eastern border of the free state [through the Compromise of 1850] of California, the very Missouri Compromise that Chief Justice Roger B. Taney

81 Lincoln believed that he needed to short-cut a New York Case, Lemmon v. People, making the right of transit of slaves permanent so long as the owner did not assume citizenship in the free state, from reaching the U.S. Supreme Court. See Gigante, "Slavery and a House Divided," at http://afroamhistory.about.com/library/prm/blhousedivided.htm; Finkelman, "The Nationalization of Slavery," 213-40, especially 221-33. See also, James M. McPherson, "What Caused the Civil War?" *North & South*, 4 (November 2000), 12-22; Jeffrey R. Hummel, "Why Did Lincoln Choose War?" *ibid.*, 4 (September 2001), 38-44; Webb Garrison, *Lincoln's Little War* (Nashville: Rutledge Hill Press, 1997).

82 Rhodehamel and Taper (eds.), *Writings of John Wilkes Booth*, 62.

had declared to be an unconstitutional denial of slavery's guaranteed extraterritoriality just three and a half years earlier.[83]

But it underlined Booth's reasonable Unionism in 1860-61, and his agreement with the position of the Constitutional Union Party, once the anti-immigrant American Party (or Know-Nothings) and before that the Whigs, which was strong in Maryland. According to his sister, Asia, Booth was a party member. In 1860, this made John Wilkes Booth a cooperationist, not a secessionist —a pro-Union Southerner in political theory.[84]

---

83 William L. Richter, *Historical Dictionary of the Civil War and Reconstruction* (Lanham, Md.: Scarecrow Press, 2004), 167-68, for Crittenden's Compromise.

84 Asia Booth Clarke, *John Wilkes Booth: A Sister's Memoir* (Ed. by Terry Alford, Jackson: University Press of Mississippi, 1996), 75, talks of Booth's attachment to the "Know Nothings" or the American Party. On the American Party, The Constitutional Union Party, and the Election of 1860, see Richter, *Historical Dictionary of the Civil War and Reconstruction*, 43-45, 156, 199-202. On Cooperators and their influence on the sectional crisis, see William L. Richter, *Historical Dictionary of the Old South* (Lanham, Md.: Scarecrow Press, 2005), introduction, 6-11.

In spite of aiding the Confederacy by running the blockade with drugs and possibly armed conflict (railroad sabotage in northern Maryland as early as 1861 is suggested in William Hanchett, *John Wilkes Booth and the Terrible Truth about the Civil War* [Racine: Lincoln Fellowship of Wisconsin, Historical Bulletin No. 49], 9-10, utilizing

"The South is leaving us," Booth groaned painfully.

"Weep fellow countrymen, for the brightest half of our

research first developed by Arthur Loux), Booth would not secede from the Union until November 1864, when he wrote his "To Whom It May Concern Letter." See Rhodehamel and Taper (eds.), *Writings of John Wilkes Booth*, 124-127, 128n.3.

Booth would justify assassinating the president in his "Letter to the Editors of the *National Intellegencer* newspaper, April 14, 1865," which, contrary to standard histories, was more than a restatement of the "To Whom It May Concern Letter." See *ibid.*, 147-53 and footnotes.

The argument over the letter's existence and its contents is in Terry Alford, "John Matthews: A Vindication of the Historical Consensus," Dillon (ed.), *The Lincoln Assassination: From the Pages of the* Surratt Courier, I, 43-47, and Deirdre Barber, "Further Thoughts on John Matthews," *ibid.*, I, 41-42, that such a letter existed, although Robert L. Mills, "John Matthews A Liar?" *ibid.*, I, 39, is not so sure. In the end, Shaffer accuses Alford of over-kill and criticizing him for points he never made, (see Thomas Shaffer, "A Final Say on John Matthews," *ibid.*, I, 49-50.But much of their argument really begs the question, as Laurie Verge states in her appended paragraphs to "A Final Say."

Actor or not, it is difficult to believe that Matthews could "wing it" and remember the intricacies of Booth's political mind. It is possible, as pointed out by James O. Hall, "That Letter to the *National Intelligencer*," Dillon (ed.), *The Lincoln Assassination: From the Pages of the* Surratt Courier, I, 33-38, that Matthews remembered the *gist* of the latter and reconstructed it years later, relying on the by then public "To Whom It May Concern" letter that Booth had stored in brother-in-law John "Sleepy" Clarke's safe.

stars upon the nation[']s banner have grown dim."[85] But, as William Shakespeare reminded us nearly three hundred years before Booth was born, "[t]he fault, dear Brutus, is not in our stars, but ourselves. . . ."[86]

H.L. Mencken put it a little differently. "The [S]outherner, at his worst, is never quite the surly cad that the Yankee is. His sensitiveness may betray him into occasional bad manners, but in the main he is a pleasant fellow—hospitable, polite, good-humored, even jovial. But a bit absurd . . .

a bit pathetic." Thomas Sowell would add lazy [we would prefer "deliberate"], lawless, and sexually immoral.[87]

So there you have him, straight out of the Sahara of the Bozart, John Wilkes Booth, at times hospitable, good-humored, jovial, absurd, pathetic, lawless, deliberate in his actions to the point of being slow,[88] ever sexually

---

85 Rhodehamel and Taper (eds.), *Writings of John Wilkes Booth*, 58.

86 *Julius Caesar*, Act I, Scene ii, Lines 140ff.

87 Mencken, "The Sahara of the Bozart," *New York Evening Mail* of November 13, 1917; Sowell, *Black Rednecks and White Liberals*, 3-27 especially 6. See also, Grady McWhiney, *Cracker Culture: Celtic Ways in the South* (University, Ala.: University of Alabama Press, 1988), for more in a similar vein heavily relied on by Sowell.

88 The slowness of civilian operatives is a constant theme in Confederate secret service operations, see, e.g., William L. Richter, *The Last Confederate Heroes* (2 vols., Laurel, Md.:

immoral, and an occasional political thinker, a self-professed Northerner who was always a Southerner, but tragically, a bygone American in his own time--an ardent defender and ideologue of the old pre-Civil War Union.

Burgundy Press, 2008, rev. ed), a novel of the Lincoln Assassination that contains more truth than fiction, *passim*, especially I, 354.

III.

"Killing a Man Is Murder, _Unless_ You Do It to the Sound of Trumpets": The Wartime Political Thought of John Wilkes Booth

Nothing mystifies the American public and the social science profession so much as why John Wilkes Booth assassinated America's most beloved president, Abraham Lincoln, the man who gave the nation a hallowed New Birth of Freedom. Lincoln was seemingly so pure in motive, so wise in his administration, so generous in his emancipation of the down-trodden black slaves, that the Confederacy and its most infamous effigy, John Wilkes Booth, have suffered the ultimate ignominy as the representative and personification of the worst insanity in American history in all of its malefic ramifications.

The common assumption that would-be Confederate hero John Wilkes Booth was not wholly sane is based on a multitude of Freudian-like reasons. Modern psychologists assert that Booth killed the president because Lincoln allegedly represented the absentee father Booth hated for his illegitimacy;[1] or perhaps he had a deep-seated Oedipal urge to impress a mother, who spoiled him incessantly;[2] or maybe he had a need to rise above his older brothers, who were arguably better actors than he.[3]

From Richard Lawrence, who fired two single-shot pistols point blank at Andrew Jackson's chest, only to have both misfire, to John Hinckley, Jr., whose six revolver shots nearly killed Ronald Reagan and seriously wounded several of his entourage, Americans have preferred their presidential assassins, whether failed or successful, to be more or less crazy. This absolves us of having to wonder where the American experiment might have gone wrong. [4]

Even if Booth is given credit for organizing his own compact murder conspiracy without the psychological innuendos,[5] he is dismissed as a "vulgar cut-throat,"

1 George W. Wilson, "John Wilkes Booth: Father Murder," *American Imago*, 1 (1940), 49-60.

2 Barbara Lerner, "The Killer Narcissists," *National Review On-line*, May 19, 1999, at townhall.com.

3 Philip Weissman, "Why Booth Killed Lincoln: A Psychoanalytic Study," *Psychoanalysis and the Social Sciences*, 5 (1958), 99-115.

4 See, *e.g.*, the statement of Joseph Bradley, Sr., in defense of accused conspirator John Surratt, Jr., quoted in Wilson, *John Wilkes Booth: Fact and Fiction of Lincoln's Assassination* (Boston: Houghton Mifflin Co., 1929), vii.

5 Michael Kauffman, *American Brutus: John Wilkes Booth and the Lincoln Assassination* (New York: Random House, 2004); Diana L. Rubino, *A Necessary End* (Unpublished ms.); Timothy Crouse, "A Conspiracy Theory to End All

leading a "Gang of Cartoon Assassins" in a morbid thirst for notoriety.[6] Moreover, Booth is further condemned as a "frustrated ham actor" who lost his stage voice because of poor speaking technique, a lecherous libertine who wound up deathly ill and out of his mind from raging syphilis, and an overbearing egotist fearful of "becoming a nobody."[7]

Conspiracy Theories: Did John Wilkes Booth Act Alone?" *Rolling Stone*, 216 (July 1, 1976), 42-44, 47, 91-92, 94.

6   Isaac Markens, "President Lincoln and the Case of John Yates Beall," http://www.geocities.com/Athens/5568/jyb.html. See also, William A. Tidwell, "John Wilkes Booth and John Yates Beall," *Surratt Courier*, 25 (November 2000), 3-5; and J. Ninian Beall, "Why Booth Killed Lincoln," Columbia Historical Society of Washington, D.C., *Records*, 48-49 [1946-47], 127-41.

7   More general materials from the preceding three paragraphs are from William Hanchett, *The Lincoln Murder Conspiracies . . .* (Urbana: University of Illinois Press, 1983), 35-58; Constance Head, "John Wilkes Booth as Hero Figure," *Journal of American Culture*, 5 Fall 1982), 22-28; Philip Van Doren Stern, *The Man Who Killed Lincoln: The Story of John Wilkes Booth and His Part in the Assassination* (New York: The Literary Guild of America, 1939) (outmoded); James McKinley, *Assassination in America* (New York: Harper & Row, 1977), 10 (misguided or deluded hero), 28; Kauffman, *American Brutus*; Francis Wilson, *John Wilkes Booth*, ix-x (vulgar, notoriety); Lloyd Lewis, *The Assassination of Lincoln: History and Myth* (Lincoln, Neb.: Bison Books, 1994, orig., 1929), 158-74 (cartoon assassinations); Larry Starkey, *Wilkes Booth Came to Washington* (New York: Random House, 1976) (Beall); James W. Clarke,

Many others prefer to see Booth a mere, thoughtless, racist cog in the wheel of a vast conspiracy masterminded by Confederate leaders,[8] or the independently-organized Knights of the Golden Circle,[9] or Northern Radical

---

American Assassins, 18-19 (ham actor); Stanley Kimmel, *The Mad Booths of Maryland* (2nd ed., rev. and enlarged, New York: Dover Publications, 1969), 262 (Booth's voice, fear of becoming a nobody). The quarrel over Booth's possibly having syphilis is in David Dillon (ed.), *The Lincoln Assassination: From the Pages of the Surratt Courier* (13 parts, Clinton, Md.: The Surratt Society, 2000), XIII, 7-14. The chronic hoarseness and sore throat could have come from a ill-advised winter journey across Missouri in the snow during the dead of winter, rather than poor voice projection, see John Rhodehamel and Louise Taper (eds.), *Writings of John Wilkes Booth* (Urbana: University of Illinois Press, 1997), 97-98n.5.

8   Hanchett, *The Lincoln Murder Conspiracies*, 59-89; Benn Pittman (comp.), *The Assassination of President Lincoln and the Trial of the Conspirators* (Cincinnati: Moore, Wilstach & Baldwin, 1865), particularly the testimony of Charles Dunham, Richard Montgomery and Dr. James B. Merritt; Francis Wilson, *John Wilkes Booth: Fact and Fiction of Lincoln's Assassination* (Boston: Houghton Mifflin Co., 1929), ix-x ; Starkey, *Wilkes Booth Came to Washington*; William A. Tidwell, James O. Hall, and David Winfred Gaddy, *Come Retribution: The Confederate Secret Service and the Assassination of Lincoln* (Jackson: University Press of Mississippi, 1988).

9   Izola Forrester, *This One Mad Act . . . : The Unknown Story of John Wilkes Booth and His Family* (Boston: Hale, Cushman, & Flint, 1937), vii. On the Knights of the Golden Circle and Southern filibustering expeditions, consult Robert E. May, *The Southern Dream of a Caribbean*

Republican politicians[10] and certain members of Lincoln's

Empire, 1854-1861 (Baton Rouge: Louisiana State University Press, 1973), 3, 20, 49, 91-94, 148-55; Olliger Crenshaw, "The Knights of the Golden Circle," *American Historical Review*, 47 (1941), 23-50; C. A. Bridges, "The Knights of the Golden Circle: A Filibustering Fantasy," *Southwestern Historical Quarterly*, 287-302; Joe A. Stout, Jr., *The Liberators: Filibustering Expeditions into Mexico, 1848-1862, and the Last Gasp of Manifest Destiny* (Los Angeles: Westernlore Press, 1973), and Stout, *Schemers and Dreamers: Filibustering in Mexico, 1848-1862* (Ft. Worth: Texas Christian University, 2002. Both Booth and neighbor T. William O'Laughlen (if not his brother Mike, too, later a co-conspirator against Lincoln) were rumored to be members of the Golden Circle. See also, Warren Getler and Bob Brewer, *Shadow of the Sentinel: One Man's Quest to Find the Hidden Treasure of the Confederacy* (New York: Simon and Schuster, 2003).

10 See Charles Higham, *Murdering Mr. Lincoln: A New Detection of the 19th century's Most Famous Crime* (Beverly Hills: New Millennium Press, 2004); and Leonard F. Guttridge and Ray A. Neff, *Dark Union: the Secret Web of Profiteers, Politicians, and Booth Conspirators that Led to Lincoln's Death* (Hoboken, N.J.: Weilet, 2003).

own cabinet,[11] or even the Jesuit order of the Roman Catholic Church.[12]

But as Confederate diplomat James Mason (of Mason and Slidell fame), noted shortly after Booth assassinated Lincoln, if Booth had acted alone, he would have been mad, but he was not—mad men seldom act in conspiracies and collaborations. [13] And sure enough,

---

11 Hanchett, *The Lincoln Murder Conspiracies*, 158-84, 210-33; Otto Eisenschiml, *Why Was Lincoln Murdered?* (New York: Grossett & Dunlap, 1937); *In the Shadow of Lincoln's Death* (New York: Wilfred Funk, 1940); Robert H Fowler, "Was Stanton Behind Lincoln's Murder [Ray Neff on L.C. Baker]," *Civil War Times Illustrated*, 3 (Aug. 1961), 4-13, 16-23, and his "New Evidence in [the] Lincoln Murder Conspiracy," *ibid.*, 7 (Feb. 1965), 4-6, 8-11; Theodore Roscoe, *The Web of Conspiracy: The Complete Story of the Men Who Murdered Lincoln* (Englewood Cliffs: Prentice-Hall,1959); Vaughn Shelton, *Mask for Treason: The Lincoln Murder Trial* (Harrisburg: Stackpole Books, 1965); David Balsiger and Charles E. Sellier, *The Lincoln Conspiracy* (Los Angeles: Schick Sunn Classic Books, 1977).

12 Hanchett, *The Lincoln Murder Conspiracies*, 233-41; Charles Chiniquy, *Fifty Years in the Church of Rome* (rev. and complete ed., London: Robert Banks & Son, [1886]; Burke McCarthy, *The Suppressed Truth about the Assassination of Abraham Lincoln* (Philadelphia: Burke McCarthy, 1924); Emmett McLoughlin, *An Inquiry into the Assassination of Abraham Lincoln* (New York: Lyle Stuart, Inc., 1963; T. M. Harris, *Assassination of Lincoln* . . . (Boston: American Citizen Co., 1892).

13 James Mason to A. Dudley Mann, April 29, 1865, in Virginia Mason (comp. and ed.), *The Public Life and Diplomatic Correspondence of James M. Mason, with Some Personal History by*

contrary to the usual historical picture, as evidenced by his first political testament, the never-publicized Philadelphia Speech, Booth's political thought at the beginning of the Civil War was fairly sophisticated and in agreement with the Constitutional Union Party's moderate position. "[The South] must be brought back [into the Union] and it must be done with compromise," he said. This reasonable Unionism in 1860 made John Wilkes Booth a cooperationist, not a secessionist—a pro-Union Southerner in political theory.[14]

But as the war progressed, Booth became more and more disillusioned with Abraham Lincoln's decisive, highly controversial, innovative, and largely Unconstitutional actions as president (among them emancipation), which Booth saw as classic expressions of imperial tyranny. Lincoln repeatedly circumvented Congress, acting through presidential proclamations whenever Congress was out of session. He then presented his independent actions as accomplished and irrevocable acts for congressional approval after the fact.[15]

Virginia Mason (New York and Washington: Neale Publishing Company, 1906), 562.

14 See William L. Richter, "Out of the Sahara of the Bozart: The Pre-war Political Thought of John Wilkes Booth," *supra*, 79-124.

15 See William L. Richter, "How Anakin Skywalker Became Darth Vader: The Abraham Lincoln John Willkes Booth Knew," *supra*, 7-78.

Booth began to show his opposition to Lincoln's war by snippy acts of protest. In Buffalo, he smashed a window containing Confederate relics of war picked up off the battlefields by local soldiers. In St. Louis, he associated with actors known for pro-Confederate sympathies, including his own sometime brother-in-law and local theater manager, Ben DeBarr, and openly condemned the Union government to hell.

In New Orleans, he was caught singing the forbidden Confederate song, "The Bonnie Blue Flag," on a public street. He talked his way out of all these offenses or paid a fine to avoid jail. In Montreal, Lower British Canada, however, Booth got a freebie. Much to the chagrin of Union spies, he led the occupants of his whole hotel in a noisy rendition of the notorious anti-Yankee song, "Maryland, My Maryland." There was no official British reaction or sanction. [16]

Just how much more Booth was willing to do for the Confederate cause is debatable. There is suspicion that he

---

16 Booth's troubles with the Yankee military authorities are presented Gordon Samples, *Lust For Fame: The Stage Career of John Wilkes Booth* (Jefferson, N.C.: McFarland & Co., 1982), 134-48; Stanley Kimmel, *Mad Booths of Maryland* (2d rev. ed. and enlarged, New York: Dover Publications, 1969), 175, and Higham, *Murdering Mr. Lincoln*, 114. On Booth's life in 1864, in general, see Constance Head, "John Wilkes Booth: Prologue to Assassination, *Lincoln Herald*, 85 (Winter 1983), 254-79.

was allied with John Merryman and the numerous raiders who destroyed or tried to burn various railroad bridges into Baltimore from the north and isolate Maryland's largest city and nearby Washington, D.C., from Union control.[17]

Others, including his sister Asia, believed that he was instrumental in running drugs into the Confederacy, especially the critical quinine that allowed armies to operate in the malarial South.[18] Still others, more imaginatively, see Booth as setting up and operating his own "French Connection" to guarantee him a constant supply of drugs, which he smuggled personally across the lines into Confederate-held territory, or delegated

---

17 The railroad sabotage is suggested in William Hanchett, *John Wilkes Booth and the Terrible Truth about the Civil War* (Racine: Lincoln Fellowship of Wisconsin, Historical Bulletin No. 49), 9-10, utilizing research first developed by Arthur Loux.

18 Asia Booth Clarke, *John Wilkes Booth: A Sister's Memoir* (Ed. by Terry Alford, Jackson: University Press of Mississippi, 1996), 85-86. See also, William A. Tidwell, James O. Hall and David Winfred Gaddy, *Come Retribution: The Confederate Secret Service and the Assassination of Lincoln* (Jackson: University Press of Mississippi, 1988), 259-60, for more on Booth's drug smuggling. For Merryman, see *ex parte* Merryman, Fed. Cases No. 9, 487 (1861) at 439.

the activity to underlings like Lincoln Assassination co-conspirator David E. Herold.[19]

But Lincoln's re-election in 1864, as his brother Edwin would theorize, was the last straw for Johnny. It was an especially cutting blow. Not only had the average Northern balloter let him down, but even brother June had actively supported Lincoln's re-election. And the normally apolitical Edwin admitted that he was proud to have actually voted for Lincoln, making Edwin the first Booth to cast a ballot in any American election—much to Johnny's horror.[20]

---

19 The French trip is covered in F. Lauriston Bullard, "When--If Ever--Was John Wilkes Booth in Paris?" *Lincoln Herald*, 50 (June 1948), 28-34; and Bullard, "A Plausible Solution of the Mystery of John Wilkes Booth's Alleged Visit to Paris," *ibid.*, 52 (October 1950), 41-43.

20 Alford (ed.), *John Wilkes Booth: A Sister's Memoir by Asia Booth Clarke*, 81, 88-89, 113, 116, 119, 121; Smith, *American Gothic*, 102-103.

   Wilson, *John Wilkes Booth*, 38-61, remarks on Johns "secession froth," and doubts that Ned or any family member would have thought enough of Johnny's letters or plots do much more than ridicule them. Booth's concept of Lincoln as Tyrant was a common theme North and South, even within the Republican Party. See *e.g.*, James W. Clarke, *American Assassins: The Darker Side of Politics* (Princeton: Princeton University Press, 1982), 26-27; Frank Klement, "A Small Town Editor Criticizes Lincoln: A Study in Editorial Abuse," *Lincoln Herald*, 54 (Summer 1952), 27-32, 60; and especially, Joseph George, Jr., "'Abraham Africanus I': President Lincoln Through the Eyes of a Copperhead Editor," *Civil War History*, 14 (September 1968), 226-41.

Johnny had long since begun humming and singing the current, derogatory folk tune, "When Lincoln Shall Be King."[21] Now, in November 1864, as Lincoln earned his second term (the first time in American history that any Northerner had been elected to two terms in a row as president), Johnny took pen to paper and produced a second political statement, the "To Whom It May Concern" letter.[22]

Booth used the impersonal opening in his letter to mimic Lincoln's use of the same phrase when the president had cavalierly refused to treat seriously with Confederate peace representatives at Niagara Falls in the autumn of

---

For the constant hostility of John Wilkes Booth and others toward those who occupied Maryland for the Union, see Charles B. Clark, "Suppression and Control of Maryland, 1861-1865: A Study of Federal-State Relations During Civil Conflict," *Maryland Historical Magazine*, 54 (September 1959)," 241-71.

21　Booth's penchant to whistle, hum, or sing forbidden songs, often to the embarrassment of his companions, is in David Miller DeWitt, *Assassination of Abraham Lincoln* (New York: Macmillan, 1909), 9.

22　On Booth's theme, "When Lincoln Shall Be King," the work of Thomas J. DiLorenzo, "The Great Centralizer: Abraham Lincoln and the War Between the States," *Independent Review*, 3 (No. 2, Fall 1998), 243-71, and *The Real Lincoln*, 54-84, are instructive. The idea that Lincoln was a tool of New England is prominent in Kevin Phillips, *The Cousins' Wars: Religion, Politics, and the Triumph of Anglo-America* (New York: Basic Books, 1999), passim. Rhodehamel and Taper (eds.), *Writings of John Wilkes Booth*, 128n.3.

1864, which had irritated Booth to no end. As usual, whenever he took pen to paper, Booth confessed, "there is no time for words. I write in haste."

As he began to record, Booth dismissively addressed his brother-in-law, John Sleeper Clarke, noted comedian and husband of Booth's favorite sister, Asia, as "My Dear Sir," and invited Clarke to "use this [letter] as you may think best. . . ."

"[I h]ave loved the Union beyond expression," Booth continued. "For four years have I waited, hoped and prayed, for the dark clouds to break, [a]nd for a restoration of our former sunshine[--]to wait longer would be a crime."[23]

As much as Booth believed that the Union was created for whites, to the exclusion of blacks, he quickly endeavored to put the issue of slavery outside the pale of discussion. He called slavery "one of the greatest blessings (both for [blacks] and [whites alike])," and claimed his view of the current war was from the same stand-point as that "held by those noble framers of our Constitution."

Yet in a letter to his mother at the same time, Booth himself evidenced a greater sympathy for the evils of slavery in the abstract than one might suppose. "For four years," he wrote, "I have lived (I may say) [a] *slave* in the [N]orth ([a] favored slave it is true, but no less

23 *Ibid.*, 124 (love peace), 126 (how I, four years).

hateful to me on that account)." Booth claimed that he had felt so constricted in his liberty that "[I dared not] to express my thoughts or sentiments, even in my own home[, c]onstantly hearing every principle, dear to my heart, denounced as treasonable."

Booth admitted that his open support of the Confederacy broke his promise to his mother not to get involved with the war. But, he said, he could no longer stand it. "[I have] cursed my willful idleness, and begun to deem myself a coward, and to despise my own existence, . . . mostly for your own . . . sake, . . . dear Mother." The outspoken Booth then hoped that "I have your forgiveness[," as he went forward to help the Confederacy], "even though you differ with me . . . in opinion."[24]

But the "South *are not, nor have they been fighting* for the continuance of slavery," Booth went on in his "To Whom It May Concern" letter. "Slavery as an issue had been done away with since the first Battle of Bull Run," Booth said. "The South's causes *since* for *war* have been as *noble*, and *greater* [by] *far*[,] *than those that* urged our [*Founding F*]*athers on*.

"*Even* should we allow [the South] were *wrong* at the beginning of this contest, [Yankee] *cruelty and injustice* have made the wrong become the *right*," Booth

---

24 *Ibid.*, 130.

maintained. The Rebels "stand now, before the wonder and admiration of the world[,] as a noble band of patriotic heroes. Hereafter, reading of *their deeds*, [that valiant last stand of Leonidas and the Spartans at] Thermopylae will be forgotten," Booth concluded.

As the war progressed, Booth continued, "I have studied hard to discover upon what grounds, the rights of a state to [s]ecede [can] been denied, when our very name (United States) [Booth used it in the plural, less binding form, common before the Civil War] and our Declaration of Independence, *both* provide for secession."[25] (By the way, one is gratified to see at least Booth had finally learned to spell "secession" and "secede" correctly, unlike in his earlier missives).[26]

Booth ruefully admitted that he had fallen for those Southern cooperationists in 1861 who had cautioned, "'Await an overt act.' Yes[,] till you are bound and plundered," Booth spat bitterly. "What folly[--]the [Lower and Upper] South were wise [to have seceded when they did]."[27]

---

25 This plural reference is explained in general in Forrest McDonald, *States' Rights and the Union: Imperium in Imperio, 1776-1876* (Lawrence: University of Kansas Press, 2000), 10, 22.

26 Rhodehamel and Taper (eds.), *Writings of John Wilkes Booth*, 125 26.

27 *Ibid.*, 124.

"How I have loved the *old flag* can never, now, be known," a dejected Booth moped. But the "blood and death" of war has "spoil[ed] her beauty and tarnish[ed] her honor, . . . til now (in my eyes) her once bright red stripes look like *bloody gashes* on the face of Heaven."

Booth then pledged, as "God is my judge, I love *justice*, more than I do the country that disowns it." Because of this, Booth said, "[m]y love (as things stand today) is for the South alone." For this love, Booth was willing to give up family, friends, happiness, fortune, and the old pre-Civil War Union, itself.

At that point, Booth made one of his most noted statements. "Right or wrong, God judge me, not man. For be my motive good or bad," Booth declared, "of one thing I am sure, the lasting condemnation of the [N]orth.

"[So] I go penniless to [the Southern] side," Booth emoted, "to triumph or die. . . ." Then he signed his letter, "*A Confederate* doing duty *upon his own responsibility*." John Wilkes Booth had seceded from the Old Union at last, three and a half years late.[28]

Just as familial and national division had brought armed conflict between the sections, Booth's personal secession brought the reality of war to him. He wrote his

28 *Ibid.*, 126 (God is), 127 (a Confederate).

rationale of assassination in his third political epistle, the April 14, 1865, letter "To My Countrymen" addressed to one of the editors, probably John F. Coyle, of the *National Intelligencer* newspaper in Washington, D.C.[29]

But there is a real problem with this document. While historians are sure Booth wrote the other letters explaining his political philosophy, this final one is usually presented as a restatement of the "To Whom It May Concern" letter. That is because Booth supposedly gave the communication to his actor friend John Matthews to mail on the morning of April 15, the day after the assassination, if Booth did not stop him before.

Upon hearing of Lincoln's death and Booth's complicity in it, Matthews suddenly remembered the letter was still in his coat pocket. He broke it open in a panic and read Booth's justification of tyrannicide. Matthews was horrified that he might be implicated in Lincoln's death and burned the pages immediately. Sometime later, during the trial of Lincoln assassination co-conspirator John H. Surratt, Jr., Matthews tried to reconstruct the missive from memory, relying on his ability as an actor to memorize such a lengthy piece after a glance or two. In other words, in theater parlance, Matthews "winged it."

---

29 The text of the letter appears in several places. See *e.g.*, *ibid.*, 147-53 and footnotes.

This has led to a quarrel among historians and people of the time as to how successful Matthews was in his recall. The text of the letter appears in several places.[30] But since Matthews supposedly burned the original document it has become traditional to say, as he claimed, that it was much the same as Booth's earlier "To Whom It May Concern" letter that had been ensconced in John Sleeper Clarke's safe in Philadelphia.

But was it? Historian Robert L. Mills[31] is not even sure the letter ever existed. He points out that we only have Matthews' own word (after all, fellow actors did not know him as "Crazy John" for nothing)[32] as to the letter's existence, and, unless Booth was "an idiot," or somehow downright "incompetent" (and we now have Michael Kauffman's book alleging the "American Brutus" had a fully capable, lay, legal mind),[33] Booth would never have given Matthews a letter, Mills asserts, that could have been used to indict him for an "unattempted murder" had he not assassinated Lincoln that Good Friday evening. Mills believes that Matthews made up the letter's existence and

---

30 See *e.g.*, *ibid.*

31 Robert L. Mills, "John Matthews A Liar?" in Douglas Dillon (ed.), *The Lincoln Assassination: From the Pages of the Surratt Courier* (13 parts in 2 vols., Clinton, Md.: Surratt Society, 2000), I, Part 1, 39.

32 Deirdre Barber, "Further Thoughts on John Matthews," Dillon (ed.), *ibid.*, I, Part 1, 41.

33 Kauffman, *American Brutus*, 172-73, 185, 359-60.

took the content from Booth's earlier "To Whom It May Concern" letter under pressure from unnamed "powerful men with leverage against him" to avoid prosecution for "suborning treason."

Unfortunately for Mills' point of view, both Booth and his traveling companion, Davy Herold, both testified as to the letter's existence. In his pocket diary, Booth mentions "a long article" that he left for one of the editors of the *National Intelligencer*, "in which I fully set forth our reasons for proceedings." Herold told Federal Judge Advocate John Bingham that Booth mentioned a letter signed by his five unnamed co-conspirators "giving their reasons for doing such and such things. . . . He said it would be in the *Intelligencer*."[34]

Like Mills, historian Thomas G. Shaffer,[35] admits that "[f]ew things can be said about Booth's letter with any certainty . . . ." On the other hand, Shaffer believes that a real letter did exist, but accuses Matthews of making up the content of the *National Intelligencer* letter out of whole cloth, because even an accomplished actor

---

34 Rhodehamel and Taper (eds.), *Writings of John Wilkes Booth*, 154; Laurie Verge (ed.), *From the War Department Files: Statements Made by the Alleged Lincoln Conspirators under Examination, 1865* (Clinton, Md.: The Surratt Society, 1980), 13-14.

35 Thomas G. Shaffer, "The Gospel According to John Matthews," Dillon (ed.), *The Lincoln Assassination: From the Pages of the* Surratt Courier, I, Part 1, 25-32.

like Matthews could not have memorized such a lengthy piece of Boothian logic in a panicked glance or two.

Matthews had hinted at the letter's existence as a witness in the 1867 impeachment proceedings against President Andrew Johnson before the House Judiciary Committee, Shaffer notes, but nobody took the bait. Later that summer, Matthews decided he had to go public with the whole matter. Matthews' purpose, Shaffer says, was to assist the defense of John Surratt, Jr., then on trial for his life as a Booth co-conspirator.

But the federal prosecutors had prevented Matthews from even saying the letter existed, as he hemmed and hawed during his testimony at the Surratt trail. So, Matthews did and end run around the court and wrote a condensed version of it and sent it to the *National Intelligencer*, Shaffer says, which published it on July 18, 1867.

Matthews made other public statements over the years and the letter, according to Shaffer, which had contained only a single page, front and back, in 1867, grew to three pages by 1878, and then ten pages, if the writing were very small, by 1881. Great memory Johnny Matthews--unlike most, it *improved* with the passage of years! And why not? The contents he gave were exactly the same as the "To Whom It May Concern" letter, well-publicized since its publication in 1865. "In all likelihood," Shaffer concluded, "John Matthews probably knew less than he revealed."

This having been said, historian and Booth biographer Terry Alford,[36] has made a convincing argument that the "Letter to the *National Intelligencer*," did exist. He says that Booth wrote *a* letter, assumed to be *the* letter, in the office of the National Hotel, according to Henry E. Merrick, the desk clerk.[37] Further, Alford points out, Booth confided to his diary that he had written and left a letter behind. Booth also told co-conspirator and fellow fugitive, Davy Herold, of its existence and was visibly disappointed, Herold said, when it did not appear in the *Intelligencer*.

In his conversation with Herold, Booth did not mention to whom exactly the letter was sent or with whom he left it, Alford said. But Booth seems to have had a political conversation with *Intelligencer* editor John F. Coyle, a well-known critic of Abraham Lincoln as president, on Good Friday morning. Alford also notes

36 Terry Alford, "John Matthews: A Vindication of the Historical Consensus," Dillon (ed.), *ibid.*, I, Part 1, 43-47.

37 This letter is more likely to be the one he sent to his mother while the National Intelligencer letter was written later that day at Deery's bar and billiard parlor above Grover's theater. See William L. Richter, *The Last Confederate Heroes* (2 vols., Laurel, Md.: Burgundy Press, 2008, rev. ed.), II, 776-77.

that a witness who owned a gymnasium across the street from Grover's Theater had seen Booth and Matthews conversing in the square that afternoon. So Matthews could have received the letter as he maintained.

But John Coyle is a better suspect, suggests Deirdre Barber,[38] agreeing with an earlier assertion by Thomas G. Shaffer. Barber points out that Coyle's role was delineated in a London, England, theater magazine's gossip column many years later.

According to the story, Coyle and four others were at a dinner party, April 14, 1865, when news arrived that John Wilkes Booth had assassinated President Lincoln. Coyle related to the gathering how he had had a conversation with Booth that morning, Barber goes on. Booth had given him an envelope and said, "if you hear of me in twenty-four hours, publish this. If you do not hear of me in that time, destroy this."

Coyle then proceeded to draw a large envelope from his inside coat pocket, Barber relates. "Destroy it at once," came the advice. "They will hang anybody who knows about the assassination, no matter how innocently they came by their knowledge. Don't open it, . . . burn it at once." That is exactly what was done, Coyle maintained, and Barber believes his story.

---

38 Deirdre Barber, "Further Thoughts on John Matthews," Dillon (ed.), *ibid.*, I, Part 1, 41-42,

Unfortunately, Coyle had already denied knowing anything about Booth's Letter to the *National Intelligencer* when questioned at the trial of the conspirators on May 17, 1865. But then, when questioned by Acting Assistant Adjutant General Colonel John Foster a month earlier (April 21, 1865), John Matthews also said he knew nothing about such a communication. Historian James O. Hall,[39] a noted Lincoln assassination scholar, believes that both men feared being ensnared in the fate of the conspirators and sought to distance themselves from Booth by lying—an understandable reaction, Hall thinks, given the accusatory spirit of the times.

Be that as it may, Coyle chose to keep silent about the letter for years, as the London theater magazine's delayed publication of his story demonstrated, but Matthews told Coyle about the letter at least four times before 1867, something both Hall and Alford found out. Hall also notes that Matthews began to unravel as early as his testimony before the House Judiciary Committee investigating President Johnson's possible impeachment on July 1, 1867. Here, Hall believes, Matthews told the truth, that he had received Booth's letter to the *National Intelligencer* the afternoon of the day of Lincoln's assassination.

---

39 James O. Hall, "That Letter to the *National Intelligencer*," Dillon (ed.), *ibid.*, I, Part 1, 33-38.

Matthews had repeated his tale before the jurors hearing the case of John Surratt, Jr., on July 16, Hall continues. But under direct questioning of counsel, Matthews evaded any actual revelation of the letter's contents, losing much credibility. He tried to regain his reputation by relating the contents for the New York *Herald* in 1878, but flubbed it up badly, and by 1881, according to Hall, Matthews remembered the alleged *gist* of the letter and reconstructed it for newspaper reporter F.A. Burr, this time relying on the by then public "To Whom it May Concern" letter that Booth had stored in brother-in-law "Sleepy" Clarke's safe back in 1864.

In the end, Shaffer[40] accuses Alford of over-kill and criticizing him for points he never made, and Alford falls back on Hall for evidence to the contrary, which Shaffer dismisses as an unimaginative "willingness to accept anything Matthews said. . . ." But much of their argument really begs the question as Laurie Verge states in her appended paragraphs to Shaffer's broadside, pointing out that Matthews did relate his story to Coyle several times in 1865, as Alford, through Hall, maintains.

If Hall, Alford, Barber, and Shaffer are correct that there was such a letter, what might Booth have really said, if one operated under the notion that he and Matthews

---

40 See Thomas G. Shaffer, "A Final Say on John Matthews," Dillon (ed.), *ibid.*, I, Part 1, 49-50.

would not have to write the same letter twice—or was it four times?[41] What influences might have determined his political thought patterns?

Three things come to mind that influenced Booth politics at this stage of the war: the names of the Booth family's male children, Abraham Lincoln's outwardly dictatorial style of government, and the president's desire to keep the Civil War going at all cost until he had achieved his and the Republican Party's announced domestic political purposes.

As John Wilkes Booth knew from childhood, a lot of it was in his own family's names.[42] Grandfather Richard Booth may have been High Church Anglican in the mid-1700s, but the family's real last name was Bota from

---

41 Gordon Samples, *Lust for Fame: The Stage Career of John Wilkes Booth* (Jefferson, N.C.: Jefferson & Company, inc., 1982), 162-66

42 The importance of the names the Booth family gave its male children was first noted in David Miller DeWitt, The Assassination of Abraham Lincoln (New York: Macmillan, 1909), 1-3. In general, see Gene Smith, *American Gothic: The Story of America's Legendary Theatrical Family--Junius, Edwin, and John Wilkes Booth* (New York: Simon & Schuster, 1992), 17-43; and Stanley Kimmel, *Mad Booths of Maryland* (New York: Bramhall House, 1957), 340-41; George Alfred Townsend, *The Life, Crime, and Capture of John Wilkes Booth* (New York: Dick & Fitzgerald, 1865), 19-27; Francis Wilson, *John Wilkes Booth: Fact and Fiction of Lincoln's Assassination* Boston: Houghton Mifflin, 1929), 1-25.

the Portuguese. The family's original progenitor was not an Englishman, but a traveling silversmith by trade, a Wandering Jew in the sneering anti-Semitic vernacular of the times, who fled his native Lusitania for England, a step ahead of the authorities, for having criticized his monarch way too publicly, a sin that constantly plagued the Booths, generation after generation.

Richard Booth was inspired by the American Revolution, so much so, that he had tried to leave England to fight for the separating Colonies while still a teen. His father had him arrested to stop him. In revenge, Richard christened his own sons for renowned dissenters from the *status quo*. One was called Algernon Sydney. The other was named Junius Brutus.

The original Algernon Sydney, in whose appellation John Wilkes Booth's uncle was baptized, had spoken out against the centralizing tendencies of the last British monarch to claim openly the right of divine rule, the very Roman Catholic, King Charles I, some one hundred years before the American Revolution.[43] Sidney had been with

---

43　The best short treatment of Algernon Sidney is Caroline Robbins, "Algernon Sidney's *Discourses Concerning Government*: Textbook of Revolution," *William and Mary Quarterly*, Series 3, 4 (1947), 267-96; see also, Alan Craig Houston, *Algernon Sidney and the Republican Heritage in England and America*. (Princeton: Princeton University Press, 1991), and Jonathan Scott, *Algernon Sidney and the English Republic, 1623-1677* (Cambridge: Cambridge

Oliver Cromwell and the Protestant Roundheads during the English Civil War. He had favored the reforms of 1640 and 1641 that mandated triennial Parliaments, restrained royal counselors and prerogative courts, curbed illegal taxes, and reduced the use of royal emergency courts.

He supported the Nineteen Propositions, items like barring the unlawful favoring of monopoly, oppressive war taxes, billeting soldiers in private homes (later included in the 3rd Amendment of the American Bill of Rights), or permitting cavalry to ride through planted crops. Sydney also backed the Great Remonstrance, that document of 1641 that cautioned the king against arbitrary actions, trying to make the country Roman Catholic again, and appointing advisors unacceptable to Parliament.

Sydney was on the commission that tried and executed the king for treason. He objected to the king's beheading—Sydney had merely wanted him dethroned. Nonetheless, he wrote an extended essay on how to lawfully depose kings that became a guidebook for the American revolutionaries.

University Press, 1988) and his *Algernon Sidney and the Restoration Crisis, 1677-1683* (Cambridge: Cambridge University Press, 1991). In his attack on John Marshall and his aggrandizement of power through the U.S. Supreme Court after the War of 1812, Virginia Justice Spencer Roane used the pseudonym "Algernon Sydney" to make his point. See McDonald, *States' Rights and the Union*, 78.

When dictator Oliver Cromwell became king in all but name, Sydney opposed him, too. Cromwell's ire forced Sydney to flee into exile. When Cromwell died and Charles II returned to the crown in 1661, Sydney came back to England and unwisely spoke out in favor of a parliamentary Republic versus the Restoration of the monarchy. Charles had him arrested, tried for treason for executing his father, and hanged.

Charles II, with his brother and successor, James II, tried to regain the royal prerogatives lost by their father in the English Civil War through issuing the Clarendon Code. Parliament, using Sydney's essay as a guide, deposed James, invited his sister and her Protestant husband, as Mary II and William III, to take up the throne and create a new government with the king subordinate to Parliament.

By accepting the throne, William and Mary agreed to the so-called English Bill of Rights, that is, the parliamentary reforms of the 1640s that Charles I and his sons hated so vehemently. William and Mary's assumption of power was labeled the Glorious Revolution of 1688.

Like Algernon Sydney, Richard Booth's other son, Junius Brutus, had an illustrious name. But it harkened back in history to the beginning of Rome. Unlike Richard's grandson, John Wilkes Booth, who idolized Marcus Brutus, one of the assassins of Julius Caesar, grandfather Richard honored the original *Junius* Brutus as one of the five founders of the Roman Republic, the entity that Julius Caesar sought to destroy in favor of his Empire, only to fall to the sharp knives of *Marcus* Brutus and his fellow counter-revolutionaries.

As the father of his own family, Junius Brutus Booth continued to name his scions after dissenting heroes. His first-born, in America, was Junius Brutus, Jr., nicknamed June by his siblings. His ninth child, next to the last in birth order, the one destined to achieve everlasting infamy, was named John Wilkes Booth.[44] And therein lies a tale.

The historical John Wilkes, actually a distant cousin of the Booths, was what was called an Opposition or Whig politician in mid-eighteenth century England.[45] They opposed the King's Party or the Tories, who supported the so-called Robinocracy, organized and led by the first

---

44 Larry Starkey, *Wilkes Booth Came to Washington* (New York: Random House, 1976), 45-46, asserts that Grandfather Richard, who had come to America to live with the Maryland Booths, actually named Johnny after the historical John Wilkes.

45 John Wilkes and the views of the English Opposition Politicians of the eighteenth century, generally called Whigs, and of the King's Men, generally called Tories, are explained in Bernard Bailyn, *Ideological Origins of the American Revolution* (Cambridge: Harvard University Press, 1967), and his *The Ordeal of Thomas Hutchinson* (Cambridge: Harvard University Press, 1974), 196-220 .

real prime minister of England, Robert (or for short, Robin) Walpole.

Robinocracy was a form of government in which the chief minister maintained a façade of constitutional procedures, while he, in fact, monopolized the whole of governmental power. The prime minister or robinarch was a sort of a king's king, who kept himself in power by selling governmental offices, contracts, and favors to those who voted him in, epitomized by continual rising taxes on the common citizen.

The original John Wilkes opposed these taxes and the corruption they encouraged, much as America's Founding Fathers did the same. He spoke out against the general warrant, or the writ of assistance, as it was called in the colonies (which was specifically prohibited in the later 4th Amendment of the U.S. Bill of Rights). The Robinocracy had Wilkes arrested, but as a member of Parliament from Middlesex, he was immune from prosecution for speech from the floor. So the Robinocracy passed a special law against Wilkes alone, a bill of attainder (prohibited by name in Art. 9 of the U.S. Constitution of 1787), which expelled him from Parliament, and arrested him again.

This time it was for publishing an obscene poem. He was charged with slander and blasphemy and convicted. But Wilkes had already fled to the Continent, so he was declared outlaw. So popular was he with the Opposition,

Wilkes chanced a return to England. He was jailed immediately. He was elected and re-elected to Parliament four times, but never could take his seat from his jail cell.

Wilkes's arrest showed the great lengths the Robinocracy would go to shut up the Opposition. American colonists particularly, of all Englishmen, thought it demonstrated that the English Bill of Rights from the Glorious Revolution was essentially null and void. To colonial Americans, Wilkes's arrest revealed that Parliament, as the main agency and protector of the rights of Englishmen, was utterly corrupt through its selling of governmental offices, contracts, and favors.

When the monarch failed to respond to American's Declaration of Rights and Grievances petition,[46] revealing him to be supportive of the Tory-dominated Parliament's corruption of the Glorious Revolution, the colonial revolutionists issued their own Declaration of Independence in 1776 against evil King George III. Wilkes proved to the American revolutionaries, known as the Patriots or the Whigs, that they had to strike a fatal military blow against the faulty British system of government and erect

---

46 The right of petition was one of the reforms of the Glorious Revolution of 1688, poipulasrized by political activist John Lilburne, to be ignored at only great jeopardy by the powers-that-be. See Paul Jacob, "Who Is John Lilburne," *Common Sense* (July 16, 2009) @citizensincharge.org.

a new political structure in its place protected by a written document, the Articles of Confederation of 1781, and then its replacement, the Constitution of 1787. Could John Wilkes Booth do no less than his noted namesake, when confronted by tyranny?

But there were other influences important to John Wilkes Booth's political psyche in 1865. One was Abraham Lincoln's outwardly dictatorial style of government, which Booth and many others, North and South, thought aped the tyrannous British kings Charles I and James II and George III, the commoner-king Oliver Cromwell, and U.S. President Andrew Jackson, better known to his enemies (who styled themselves as American "Whigs") as "King Andrew I of Veto Memory."

Although Booth probably never heard of or read Abraham Lincoln's 1838 Speech before the Young Men's Lyceum of Springfield, Illinois, it was crucial in demonstrating the future president's mindset as to his proper role as a Whig-Republican politician in mid-nineteenth century America.[47] Entitled "The Perpetuation

---

47　The significance of Abraham Lincoln's 1838 Speech before the Young Men's Lyceum is laid out in Edmund Wilson, *Patriotic Gore: Studies in the Literature of the American Civil War* (New York: Oxford University Press, 1962), 106-108. A more recent look ad the speech is Major L. Wilson, "Lincoln and Van Buren in the Steps of the Fathers: Another Look at the Lyceum Address," *Civil War History*, 29 (September 1983), 197-211. Also important

of Our Political Institutions," Lincoln theorized how a Cromwellian or Caesarian dictatorship, led by the proverbial man on the white horse, might replace the republican form of government created by the Founding Fathers.

"Theirs was the task (and nobly they performed it) to . . . uprear . . . a political edifice of liberty and equal rights," Lincoln posited. "It is ours only, to transmit [this] . . . to the latest generation. . . . "How, then, shall we perform it?" Lincoln queried. "That our form of government should have been maintained in its original form from its establishment until now, is . . . a practical demonstration of the truth of a proposition, which had hitherto been considered, at best, no better than problematical; namely, *the capability of a people to govern themselves.*

"Now, the experiment is successful," Lincoln asserted proudly. "But . . . [i]t is to deny what the history of the world tells us is true, to suppose that men of ambition and

---

are the materials in George B. Forgie, "Lincoln's Tyrants," in Boritt and Forness (eds.), *The Historian's Lincoln*, 285-312. Forgie wonders whether Jefferson Davis and others of the same era saw a similar threat to American institutions as did Lincoln, and reacted just as dictatorially as he has been accused of doing.

The speech itself is in Roy P. Basler *et al.* (eds.), *The Collected Works of Abraham Lincoln* (9 vols., New Brunswick, N.J.: Rutgers University Press, 1953), I, 108-15.

talents will not continue to spring up amongst us. And, when they do," Lincoln warned his audience, "they will as naturally seek the gratification of their ruling passion, as others have *so* done before them.

"The question then is," Lincoln asserted, "can that gratification be found in supporting and maintaining an edifice that has been erected by others? Most certainly it *cannot*," Lincoln proclaimed. "Towering genius. . . *scorns* to tread in the footsteps of *any* predecessor, however illustrious. It thirsts and burns for distinction; and, if possible, it will have it, whether at the expense of emancipating slaves, or enslaving freemen.

"Is it unreasonable then to expect," Lincoln asked, "that some man possessed of lofty genius, coupled with ambition sufficient to push it to its utmost stretch, will at sometime, spring up among us? . . . Distinction will be his paramount object," Lincoln admonished his listeners, "and . . . [with] nothing left to be done in the way of building up, he would set boldly to the task of pulling down."

Was Lincoln that egotistical savior, that would-be dictator? Did he predict his own presidency? Did he alone possess that "cold, calculating, unimpassioned reason" that would reshape the "pillars of the temple of liberty" in his own image, by "emancipating slaves" *and* (rather than Lincoln's less inclusive *or*) "enslaving freemen" (through an increase in the power of the central government), which he would then cover-up by calling it, "A New Birth of Freedom?"

Many then and now, along with John Wilkes Booth, say "yes." Lincoln was unabashedly dictatorial as president during the war, maintained contemporaries and modern historians, as he became "our first imperial president" through his extensive use of the executive proclamation. Upon entering office, Lincoln effected many unconstitutional acts. He summoned the militia, spent unauthorized millions, sanctioned recruiting, declared the South to be in rebellion and invaded it (implying that the South had *not* seceded), decreed a Naval blockade of the South (inferring that the South *had* seceded because, according to international law, a nation cannot blockade its own coastline), defied the Supreme Court, and pledged the nation's credit.

As Booth and critics, then and now, of the Lincoln presidency decried, Lincoln furthermore suspended the writ of habeas corpus, declared martial law, established new units of government, appointed military officers to rule over the conquered sections of the South, confiscated private property and firearms, imprisoned dissenters without trial (arresting as many as 20,000 and putting them in a Yankee "Gulag" or Concentration Camp), closed over 300 newspapers critical of his wartime actions (10%

of all those published in the North), censored telegraphic transmissions, nationalized private railroads, imported at least 500,000 foreign mercenaries (immigrants) to fight his war, deported an opposing member of Congress, and interfered with Federal troops in local and national elections in 1864 that guaranteed emancipation in Maryland and Missouri and garnered him a second term (when 38,000 votes might have changed the result).

Finally, he gutted the Ninth and Tenth Amendments to the Constitution, which guaranteed the inherent rights of the states and the people; made a new state, West Virginia, out of an old one using creative constitutional theories for five electoral votes in 1864; broke Nevada off from polygamous Mormon Utah Territory, when it lacked the statutorily required population to make it a territory (much less a state), for three more electoral votes in 1864; and cavalierly dismissed it all as "expedient."[48]

Even more "expedient" to Booth and history was Lincoln's role as military leader, which one commentator defined as "commander and selector of Northern generals, chief commissary of Federal forces, and head of government in dealing with the leaders of an opposing power." Yet, rather than stand up for the people's and its

---

48 M. E. Bradford, "The Lincoln Legacy: A Long View," in his *Remembering Who We Are: Reflections of a Southern Conservative* (Athens: University of Georgia Press, 1985), 149-50.

own guaranteed rights under the Constitution, Congress passed an indemnity act to declare all presidential, cabinet, and military actions valid in 1863. The measure passed the House of Representatives but not the Senate. The presiding officer of the Senate was up to the task--he simply declared it enacted without a vote count.

Historians, as did Booth, have long recognized Lincoln as an elected dictator, but usually they have tempered their notice by calling him a good, great, or necessary one—something Booth the constitutional purist would have scoffed at. Lincoln scholars find that his presidential proclamations saved the Union in spite destroying much of the Constitution. Those who disagree with this view are dismissed as "extremists." Indeed, one modern Lincoln defender, Clinton Rossiter, wrote a book entitled *Constitutional Dictatorship*, without realizing what a contradiction in terms that implied. [49]

This much about Lincoln, Booth understood. But there was more about the sixteenth president that Booth probably never even dreamed. According to historians critical of Lincoln's role as the Caesar he spoke of in his Lyceum Address, Honest Abe did his unprincipled best to keep the Civil War going at all cost until he had achieved his and the Republican Party's domestic political purposes. This, the historians have maintained,

49 DiLorenzo, *The Real Lincoln*, 5-6, 130-69.

more than dictatorship (as Booth and civil libertarians theorized), or forced Union (as the Confederates and Northern Copperheads believed), determined Lincoln's wartime illegalities.

"It is something requiring explanation," early twentieth century Lincoln biographer and critic Edgar Lee Masters contended, "that Lincoln, who is held up as an apostle of liberty, who himself along the way said so much [about] the Declaration of Independence and [Thomas] Jefferson, turned in his youth to the rhetorician [and Whig Party leader] Henry Clay and clung to him into maturity, and followed" Clay's economic program, the American System, "essentially to the end." [50]

The American System was a political program that promoted a national banking system, internal improvements (roads, bridges, harbors, canals), and the liberation of American slaves and their return to Africa. Clay originally hoped to finance this with a high tariff designed to exclude foreign imports, which would also protect American infant industries, and the sale of land in the western territories at $1.25 an acre. But by the 1850s, the notion of land sales had evaporated in favor of homesteading the land for free, causing the rest of the program to rely on the tariff alone for its financing--a

---

50 Masters, *Lincoln, the Man,* 3, 4, 26.

tariff paid predominantly by the South, which imported European goods in exchange for its cotton.[51]

Historians call this "Lincoln's political economy," that is, his management of the commercial and business life of North that later infected the whole nation as the "Great Barbecue," or what Mark Twain cleverly labeled as the "Gilded Age," or what modern historian Mark W. Summers more bluntly calls the "Era of Good Stealings."[52] While many of the corruptions of the Republican Era came to the fore after Lincoln's death, they began under Lincoln's direction or sponsorship, under the guise of wartime "military necessity."[53]

---

51 Masters, *Lincoln, the Man*, 122, 297. For the American System, see Glyndon G. Van Deusen, *The Jacksonian Era, 1828-1848* (New York: Harper & Row, Publishers, 1959), 51.

52 Samuel Langhorne Clemens [Mark Twain] and Charles Dudley Warner, *The Gilded Age* (Hartford: American Publishing Co., 1873); Mark W. Summers, *Era of Good Stealings* (New York: Oxford University Press, 1993). See also Summers' other pieces, "'A Band of Brigands': Albany Lawmakers and Republican National Politics, 1860," *Civil War History*, 30 (1984), 101-19; *The Plundering Generation: Corruption and the Crisis of the Union* (New York: Oxford University Press, 1987); and *Railroads, Reconstruction, and the Gospel of Prosperity: Aid Under the Radical Republicans* (Princeton: Princeton University Press, 1984).

53 Wilson (ed.), *A Defender of Southern Conservatism*, 143; and M. E. Bradford, "Dividing the House: The Gnosticism of Lincoln's Political Rhetoric," *Modern Age*, 23 (Winter

Basically, in Lincoln's economic program, creditors got the upper hand over debtors of the first time since Andrew Jackson destroyed the elitist Second Bank of the United States back in 1833. The Republican government under Lincoln's leadership became the sponsor of a great transfer of wealth using first, the protective tariff on foreign imports (which rose from 18.84% in 1861 to 47.56% in 1865); second, the massive funding of internal improvements (especially the Union Pacific Railroad which led to the Crédit Mobilier scandal); third, a national banking system (that sponsored the creation of $480 million in fiat paper money to enhance credit for big business at the expense of small businesses and farms and later redeemed it from the rich at one-to-one for gold), and finally, the Homestead Act (in which less than 19% of the lands went to actual farmers, the rest to big businesses like railroads).

From the beginning, Lincoln warned his Republican cronies not to talk publicly about their views on these subjects. But like them, Lincoln "seethed in frustration" at the lack of constitutional and popular support for the American System. Lincoln's plan was a mercantile ideology, a system which used faulty economic theory

1979), 10-21, especially 20-21. See also, Bradford, "Lincoln and the Language of hate and Fear: A Southern View," in his *Against the Barbarians and Other Reflections on Familiar Themes*, 229-45.

to build empires and subsidize individuals or groups or industries favored by the state. It essentially *prevented* free trade competition and raised local prices to consumers. It was a fancy cover for corporate welfare for select industries that ultimately led to the widespread corruption of the Civil War, the Reconstruction Era that followed, and the Gilded Age all the way to Spanish American War of 1898. [54]

Lincoln, critics argue, blithely encouraged the "rotten army contracts system," "massive thefts of Southern property," allowing "special cronies and favorites of his friends to trade in Southern cotton," and a "calculated use of the patronage and the pork barrel [nowadays called earmarks]" that resulted in "almost $10 million being pumped into local Republican [political] organizations." [55]

The argument here is that the reason for a war to end slavery in the United States was to guarantee the institution of Henry Clay's American System of which Lincoln was the prime proponent in 1860. Under the cover of saving the Union, Lincoln (by executive fiat), and

54 DiLorenzo, *The Real Lincoln*, 3, 4-5, 54-84, 234.
55 M. E. Bradford, "The Lincoln Legacy: A Long View," in his *Remembering Who We Are: Reflections of a Southern Conservative* (Athens: University of Georgia Press, 1985), 146-49. See also the exchange between Bradford and Gabor S. Boritt, in Boritt (ed.), *The Historian's Lincoln: Pseudohistory, Psychohistory, and History* , 87-123.

the new Republican majority in both houses of Congress (made possible by Southern secession), could pass their economic system, blocked since 1824 by Henry Clay's political opponents, particularly from the South.

Because opposition to the American System had been centered around Southern Democrats for so long, it was imperative to keep the South out of the Union in the 1860s long enough to allow the Republican majority to enact its programs as war measures. In domestic economic policy, Lincoln was always a High Whig, not a modern capitalist as historians usually have asserted. [56]

When Union proved to be an insufficient cause to distract the public's attention from his economic system designed for the Robber Barons, Lincoln began to speak out on the slavery issue "wholly for effect," say critics, not to guarantee any civil rights for blacks. Again, he showed a sense of his own destiny as the man on the white horse he spoke of in his Lyceum Address, who would gain absolute power by *"emancipating slaves or enslaving free men."*[57]

---

56 DiLorenzo, *The Real Lincoln*, 118-19, 121, 126, 128-29.

57 Bradford, "Dividing the House: The Gnosticism of Lincoln's Political Rhetoric," *Modern Age*, 23 (Winter 1979), 10-21, especially 20-21, and his "Lincoln and the Language of hate and Fear: A Southern View," in his *Against the Barbarians and Other Reflections on Familiar Themes*, 229-45.

There he was, then, the controversial sixteenth president of the United States, whom Americans knew only too well, before John Wilkes Booth shot him into being the greatest American hero of all time. Cognizant of the influences of the family and political environment Booth grew up and lived in, and under the realization that Matthews could not conjure up an accurate letter one (1867), two (1878), or three times (1881), any more than a multitude of historians have done since, let's engage in a little historical fiction--the privilege of writing what Booth *might* have actually said once (1864), had Matthews not burned the original and befuddled history and historians since with his machinations:[58]

WASHINGTON, D.C., 14 APRIL 1865[59]

TO MY COUNTRYMEN:

FOR YEARS I HAVE DEVOTED MY TIME, MY ENERGIES, AND EVERY DOLLAR I POSSESSED TO THE FURTHERANCE

---

58 Samples, *Lust for Fame*, 162-66.
59 The letter as Matthews "remembered" it, indicated here in small capitals type, is in Rhodehamel and Taper (eds.), *Writings of John Wilkes Booth*, 147-50.
    This conjecture of Booth's real letter relies on Algernon Sidney, *Discourses Concerning Government* (Edited by Thomas G. West. Indianapolis: Library Classics, 1990); DiLorenzo, "The Great Centralizer: Abraham Lincoln and the War Between the States," 243-71, his *The Real Lincoln*; and Younger (ed.), *Inside the Confederate Government: The Diary of Robert Garlick Hill Kean*, particularly the

OF AN OBJECT [i.e., kidnapping Lincoln]. I HAVE BEEN
BAFFLED AND DISAPPOINTED. THE HOUR HAS COME WHEN
I MUST CHANGE MY PLAN. MANY, I KNOW--THE VULGAR
HERD--WILL BLAME ME FOR WHAT I AM ABOUT TO DO, BUT
POSTERITY, I AM SURE, WILL JUSTIFY ME.

THIS WAR IS A WAR WITH THE CONSTITUTIONAL AND
RESERVE[D] RIGHTS OF THE STATE[S]. IT IS A WAR UPON
SOUTHERN RIGHTS AND INSTITUTIONS. THE NOMINATION
OF ABRAHAM LINCOLN FOUR YEARS AGO BESPOKE WAR.
HIS ELECTION FORCED IT.

I HAVE EVER HELD THAT THE SOUTH WERE RIGHT. The
principles secured by the Founding Fathers through the
American Revolution are that all *white* men are created
equal; that just government rests on consent of the
governed; that government is instituted among men to
secure the indefeasible rights of human nature; that one
of these inalienable rights is the right to revolt against
despotism. Indeed, rebellion against tyranny is not a
crime but a benefaction.

---

section on how the Lincoln Administration violated the
Constitution as it stood in 1860, pp. 215-23. See also,
Edward Hyams, "Abraham Lincoln: A Victim of Faction,"
in his *Killing No Murder: A Study of Assassination as a
Political Means* (London: Panther Modern Society, 1970),
68-69; Webb Garrison, *Lincoln's Little War: How His
Carefully Crafted Plans Went Astray* (Nashville: Rutledge
Hill Press, 1997).

This right of revolution is governed by two principles: (1) when the Executive desires or attempts to govern arbitrarily and not by law or Constitution, and (2) when the Executive seeks to exercise a power that the Constitution does not grant him. By doing both, President Lincoln seeks to replace freedom of consent and law with force and slavery. The exercise of power beyond right is Tyranny.

In certain circumstances, such as those we live in now, only the force of violent revolution is capable of ensuring that the power of the president is limited and exercised according to law and not his will. Any president who so acts may be resisted by the common citizen, or a combination of many citizens, just as a body resists an invader of his property. A Tyrant replaces law with force and institutes a war between people and government, as President Lincoln did in 1861, by refusing compromise on the issue slavery in the territories, and forcing the South to fire on Ft. Sumter. And he yet had the temerity to assert in his Second Inaugural Address that he sought to *avoid* war.

Moreover, this so-called Executive, with the connivance of his party, seeks to free the slaves through executive proclamation, then by a constitutional amendment, passed through a Congress absent the representatives of the very people whom the amendment would affect. It is the only manner in which he could gain the votes necessary. He cares nothing for the future of the black people, slave or free, replacing the security and benevolence of slavery with nothing but exploitive freedom that leaves them drifting in a hostile white society with no future.

President Lincoln allows the corruption of our government by jobbers and cronies and justifies all as wartime measures necessary to defeat the Confederacy. He has instituted the unconstitutional, thieving economic program of the discredited Henry Clay, the Corrupt Bargainer of 1824, who sought to keep the great Andrew Jackson from power after he was fairly chosen by the American people. This includes high tariffs, to destroy the cotton exports of the South; controlling national banks, to destroy access of the common man to easy money; internal improvements, to the benefit of his Northern section alone; homesteading, which squanders our national legacy in the West, to attract immigrants who defile our culture and will be taught to vote Republican; and bounties for railroads, to link the North to the West at the exclusion of the South, even though military surveyors found the southern route the most practicable. All of this is financed by the highest taxes in American history, including an unconstitutional direct tax on personal incomes, designed to stifle the natural incentive of the American industrial and agricultural communities.

Worse yet, the President has *illegally and unconstitutionally* expanded the powers of the executive beyond the limits of those imposed on the office by the Founders. He summoned the militia, a right of Congress; expanded the size of the regular army, again a prerogative of Congress; decreed an illegal blockade against part of his own nation, since he refused to recognize the independence of the Confederate States; arrested unoffending citizens, denying their rights to print, assemble, and discuss political issues of the day; refused to honor the writ of *habeas corpus* and defied his own Supreme Court, particularly its Chief Justice, when asked to show where in the Constitution his power of arbitrary arrest lay; illegally transferred thousands of dollars appropriated for specific purposes by Congress to his own pet projects; and pledged the honor and credit of the United States without authority.

He put domestic priorities of creating an *infernal Republican political machine* ahead of preserving the lives and well-being of American soldiers in the field. His political considerations brought forth hundreds of incompetent officers, many of them generals, for party patronage. Each time peace has been in the offing, he has *refused* to consider it. He prefers to continue the bloodletting by raising new terms or objections or stalling and refusing to negotiate in good faith. The latest of these outrages was the Hampton Roads Conference a few weeks ago.

And why not? He *started the war* by refusing to accept fair payment for Federal installations in the South and forcing the South to fire first to preserve its own national integrity, when he tried to succor and reinforce his illegal garrison at Ft. Sumter. He *continues it* through the offices of General U.S. (or is it Useless?) Grant and his subordinates, *traduced* by the promise of future Republican political rewards. The only thing that makes this American Bastille more bearable than that of the French Revolution is the *absence* of mass executions.

The general revolt of all or a part of this Nation against these Republican travesties cannot be called the *War of the Rebellion*, as Lincoln and his minions maintain. Lincoln's use of the word "rebellion" to describe opponents of his unlawful and unconstitutional applications of power illustrates a self-aggrandizing mindset. To describe as "rebel" those who wish to *preserve* the Constitution is to stand the word on its head. It is beyond intellectually dishonest--it is mendacity.

Indeed, the term Rebel ought to be applied to the Tyrant Lincoln, not those who *resist* his unlawful and unconstitutional applications of power. But to defy a

Tyrant one must have exhausted all other forms of legal resistance. It should only be resorted to after a pattern of abuse has been established. That is, there must be more than ill-administration but actual malice in the president's actions. I was a Cooperationist in 1860, wishing to see for myself the evils this barbarian would institute. I can no longer be anything but an Opponent, a Secessionist. President Lincoln has forfeited his trust and, by needs be, his very life.

One might argue, it is one thing to destroy the Tyrant, but *quite another* to destroy the Tyranny. Mere removal of the president will leave the Constitution intact with all the weaknesses that led to his rule in the first place. All constitutions are subject to corruption over time.

But the American government was *not* ill-constituted, the defects more lately observed proceeding from the change of manners and the corruption of the times, and the desire of Lincoln and his Black Republicans to meddle with the best system of government created by man.

The purpose of this so-called Rebellion is to restore the rule of law. The Union as it was and the Constitution as it is. Constitutional government and the separation of powers were designed to guarantee this restoration by checking corruption, facilitating change, and advancing the public interest. We have always governed ourselves, and we always meant to. Lincoln did not mean that we

should. Proclamations are not laws, they are merely the opinion of the President.

It has been hitherto been thought, that to kill a King or a President was a abominable action. They who did it, were thought to be incited by the worst of passions that can enter into the hearts of men. But under the current circumstances, it must be rather the most commendable and glorious act that can be performed by man.

I say, death to Tyrants, by any means and in any way. Tyrannicide is the public duty of all good citizens. The only inconvenience is that all depends upon success, and he who tries is the worst of villains if he fail; and at best may be deprived of all by the same means he employed to gain it.

The success of the South has been dear to my heart, and I have labored faithfully to further an object which would more than have proved my unselfish devotion. Heartsick and disappointed, I turn from the path I have been following into a bolder and more perilous one. Without malice I make the change. I have nothing in my heart except a sense of duty to my choice. After all, as the ancient Roman, Tertullian, said, against men guilty of treason and against public enemies, *every man* is a soldier.

IF THE SOUTH IS TO BE AIDED, IT MUST BE DONE *QUICKLY*. IT MAY ALREADY BE *TOO LATE*. WHEN CAESAR HAD

CONQUERED THE ENEMIES OF ROME AND THE POWER THAT WAS HIS MENACED THE LIBERTIES OF THE PEOPLE, BRUTUS AROSE AND SLEW HIM. THE STROKE OF HIS DAGGER WAS GUIDED BY HIS LOVE OF ROME. IT WAS THE *SPIRIT AND AMBITION* OF CAESAR THAT BRUTUS STRUCK AT.

OH THAT WE COULD COME BY CAESAR'S SPIRIT,

AND NOT DISMEMBER CAESAR!

BUT, ALAS!

CAESAR MUST BLEED FOR IT.[60]

WE ANSWER WITH BRUTUS:

MEN WHO LOVE OUR COUNTRY BETTER THAN GOLD OR LIFE.

J. WILKES BOOTH

John H. Surratt, Jr.[61]

Lewis Payne

David E. Herold

G. Andrew Atzerodt

Whether these three documents (the missing Letter to the *National Intelligencer* of April 1865, the "To Whom It May Concern" letter of November 1864, and

---

60 *Julius Caesar*, Act II, Scene I, Lines 169-71.

61 John Matthews excluded any mention of John H. Surratt, Jr., because he was on trial of complicity in Lincoln's assassination in 1867. He was consistent in this exclusion in later versions of the letter, because Surratt had received a hung jury not a "not guilty" verdict. Here he put in where he deserves to be. This version of Booth's letter first appeared in Richter, *Last Confederate Heroes*, II, 76-80.

the never-publicized, rough-draft Philadelphia Speech of December 1860) made Booth a loner in an intimate conspiracy he developed himself, or a co-conspirator in a larger plot engineered by others, or some sort of psychotic, is irrelevant. As far as Booth was concerned, the robinarch tyrant Abraham Lincoln had to "go up the spout,"[62] as they said in those days, as a casualty of the war he started and pursued.

After all, as the French philosophe Francois-Marie Arouet Voltaire once observed, rather cynically, "Killing a man is murder, *unless* you do it to the sound of trumpets." Booth had heard the bugles—the Siren's song.

In this light, it has been the contention of historian and Lincoln Assassination scholar, William Hanchett, that we should accord Booth the "respectability of rational political motivation." Booth, Hanchett suggested, "deserves a measure of respect we so generously and indiscriminately pay to men on both sides of the war who fought, killed, and died for what they believed. When we are able to make this concession to Booth," Hanchett

---

62 Phrase from Joseph George, Jr. "Old Abe Must Go Up the Spout': Henry von Steinaecker and the Lincoln of the Lincoln Conspiracy Trial," *Lincoln Herald*, 94 (Winter 1992), 148-56.

concluded, "we will truly understand how terrible the Civil War was."[63]

Perhaps, one hundred and fifty years later, that time has finally come.

---

63 Hanchett, *John Wilkes Booth and the Terrible Truth about the Civil War*, 34-35.